MW00452835

Beatitudes for the Workplace

"As an experienced Jesuit priest with a practical background in business, a vast knowledge of morality and ethics, and a well-developed and compassionate understanding of human nature, Father Max Oliva has provided excellent, life-changing guidance to me over the years. He has greatly influenced me to make significant, lasting positive changes in my career, and in my personal life. To anyone who is searching for the truth, I highly recommend that you pick up one of his books, or attend one of his retreats. You won't be disappointed!"

—Murray D. Wolfe, CA, Director, Internal Audit & ERM

"My friendship with Father Max was my first close friendship with a priest, despite being a practising Catholic all my life. Through two commuter retreats and our monthly meetings at a local Irish pub, where we shared stories over a pint of Guinness and a good cigar, I came to a much deeper appreciation of the role of God, Jesus and especially the Holy Spirit in my professional and personal life. Father Max has reached into the hearts and souls of many business people in the Calgary business community, challenging us to live lives of courage and integrity."

—Paul Moynihan, Investment Banker

"At times I believe people's spiritual and business lives seem to be lived on separate paths. People and businesses thrive when these two paths connect. Father Max has been a wonderful source of knowledge for me and my colleagues in integrating spirituality with the practical business realities faced in our everyday business lives."

—Sue Kuethe, Petroleum Land Negotiator,
Vice-President and General Manager

"Father Max has found a way to touch the soul of business executives struggling with the day-to-day humdrum or the crises of business life. Anyone would benefit from an hour sitting with Father Max or his writings."

—Kirk O. Hanson, University Professor and Executive Director,
Markkula Center for Applied Ethics, Santa Clara University

"There are many spiritual authors and guides, but few possess Father Max Oliva's ability to explore Christian core values in the context of everyday life. Father Max's method of combining personal experience with theological knowledge has helped me to live by my spiritual values and apply them to my personal and professional decisions."

—Shirley-anne Reuben, Executive Director,
Alexandra Centre Society, Calgary, Alberta

Beatitudes
for the Workplace

Max Oliva S.J.

NOVALIS

© 2009 Novalis Publishing Inc.

Cover: Blair Turner
Layout: Audrey Wells

Business Offices:
Novalis Publishing Inc.   Novalis Publishing Inc.
10 Lower Spadina Avenue, Suite 400   4475 Frontenac Street
Toronto, Ontario, Canada   Montréal, Québec
M5V 2Z2   Canada H2H 2S2

Phone: 1-800-387-7164
Fax: 1-800-204-4140
E-mail: books@novalis.ca

www.novalis.ca

Library and Archives Canada Cataloguing in Publication

Olivia, Max, 1939-
    Beatitudes for the workplace / Max Olivia.

Includes bibliographical references.

ISBN 978-2-89646-125-7

    1. Business--Religious aspects--Christianity.
2. Businesspeople--Religious life. I. Title.

HF5388.O45 2009   261.8'5   C2009-900949-8

Printed in Canada.

All rights reserved. No part of this publication may be reproduced, stored in a retrieval system, or transmitted in any form, or by any means, electronic, mechanical, photocopying, recording, or otherwise, without the written permission of the publisher.

Unless otherwise noted, the Scripture quotations contained herein are from the New Revised Standard Version of the Bible, copyrighted 1989 by the Division of Christian Education of the National Council of the Churches of Christ in the United States of America, and are used by permission. All rights reserved.

We acknowledge the financial support of the Government of Canada through the Book Publishing Industry Development Program (BPIDP) for our publishing activities.

Dedication

In memory of Bill Spohn, good friend, moral theologian, ethics scholar, and inspiration on how to live one's final days on this earth.

To the men and women I have met in the corporate community who have freely and generously shared with me their wisdom; the challenges they face in living their spirituality in the workplace; and the sincere efforts they are making to live ethical lives both personally and professionally.

Acknowledgments

Writing a book is a collaborative effort. I am deeply grateful for the many people who have assisted me in this project. On a personal level, I wish to thank Father Larry Bagnall and the staff and parishioners of St. Mary's Cathedral in Calgary, Alberta, for their encouraging support as I wrote the book. Special thanks to the FCJ Sisters and to the following friends who supported me with both food for the body and sustenance for my spirit: Tenny Wright; Mike Smith; Robert Raspo; the Kunkle family; Maria McIver; Jocelyne Lajoie and John Mungham; Gary Spear and Shirley-Anne Reuben; the Cretin, Grainger, and La Prise families; and the Pender family.

When I began "Spirituality at Work," the title of my ministry since 2002, I sought the counsel of Bishop Frederick Henry, bishop of the Diocese of Calgary. He encouraged me to pursue this ministry. I also consulted certain experts in the field of ethics and spirituality. Here I want to acknowledge in particular the contributions of Andre Delbecq, Ed Epstein, and Kirk Hanson, Ernie McCullough and E.T. "Jeep" Hall.

In writing the book, I used three main sources: my experience as a spiritual and ethical coach, conversations with men and women in the corporate world, and books on the topics covered. In light of the second source, I want to thank the following people: Larry Buzan and the men of the Friday morning breakfast group, members of the Thursday morning and Thursday evening "Sharing the Journey" groups, Bob Campbell, Dan Doherty, Jackie Flanagan, Barry Giovanetto, David Irvine, Janet Jacques, Rosemary Johnston, Sue Kuethe, Allan Markin, Bruce and Bill (father, son) MacDonald, Paul Moynihan, Jeff Nelson, Pat O'Brien, Jim Pender, Len Rodrigues, Sano Stante, and David Stuart.

I also owe a debt of gratitude to Penny Giovanetto, my tireless proofreader, for her excellent work on the manuscript. Special thanks as well to Kevin Burns, the first editor of the book, for his insightful suggestions; to Suzanne Nussey, the copy editor; and to Anne Louise Mahoney, the managing editor, for her attention to detail.

Contents

Introduction

I come from a family of entrepreneurs. My mother's father, his brother and my father each founded companies that flourished. Starting something from scratch is in my blood.

In the summer of 2001, I was at a crossroads in my ministry. I had been on the road, giving retreats and workshops, since 1980. This ministry required much travelling; the constant changing of beds was beginning to bother my back, so I was looking for work that would keep me in one place. Before I joined the Society of Jesus (the Jesuits), I worked in business. I also have an undergraduate degree in Marketing and an MBA in Organizational Behaviour and Industrial Relations. An article entitled "God and Business" in the June 2001 issue of *Fortune* magazine led me to a new idea for ministry: offering my expertise in business and in spirituality to business people to help them see more clearly the connection between their faith and their work.

I discussed the idea for the "Spirituality at Work" ministry with a business friend of mine in Calgary, where I had recently moved. He reacted enthusiastically. "Father Max, it's a moral desert out there. We need you!" As this ministry took shape, many men and women in the corporate world became interested in it. They encouraged me, taught me, challenged me, and blessed me with their confidence in what I had to offer. They also shared their struggles to live an ethical life on a consistent basis. I have witnessed executives and those in other roles wrestling with fundamental life questions:

- What is the ultimate purpose of my existence?
- What really gives my life meaning?
- What more is there to life after a successful career?
- How do I experience the presence of God in my daily life?
- How can I better bring the light of my faith to the ethical issues I face?

In addition to the many conversations I was privileged to have during the period from 2001 to 2007, when people shared their personal stories with me, for this writing project I enlisted the aid of eighteen men and women who graciously agreed to complete a two-part questionnaire on work and spirituality.[1] Their responses were garnered by way of personal interviews conducted in each person's work milieu. Their stories, and others, are found in each chapter. These are the questions the question-naire asked them to discuss:

1. Describe a *personal* moral or ethical dilemma you have encountered, or are encountering in your work life. How did you deal with it?

What virtue(s) do you think was helpful/would be helpful in such a situation: for example, honesty, integrity, compassion, courage, fairness, humility, etc. Explain why.

2. Describe a *social* moral or ethical dilemma you have en-countered, or are encountering: for example, issues dealing with the environment, with Aboriginal people, with people who are homeless, discrimination in the workplace, global issues of justice/injustice, etc.

What virtue(s) do you think was helpful/would be helpful in such a situation: for example, honesty, integrity, compassion, courage, fairness, humility, etc. Explain why.

For the book, I chose the format of *beatitude*, which comes from the Latin word *beatus*, meaning blessedness or happiness. I used this approach for a couple of reasons. First, this form of teaching by Jesus in the Gospels (see Matthew 5:1-11) has fascinated me for many years. I have prayed over the Beatitudes, given retreats on them, even written a book on these gems of wisdom.[2] Second, the first part of this new century has been rocked by corporate ethical scandals in both Canada and the United States. As a result, many people lost their connection to their moral compass. Jesus' message in the Beatitudes reaches to the core of ethical conduct.

According to scripture scholar Father John McKenzie, "A beatitude is a declaration of blessedness on the ground of some virtue or good fortune."[3] I have taken this literary form of beatitude and applied it specifically to the workplace, both to celebrate the good that is being done by men and women in their work environment and to encourage those who sincerely wish to live their values in a world that can be hostile to those living an honourable life. I frame the conversation around eight virtues:

- wisdom
- integrity
- honesty
- compassion for others
- justice for the earth
- forgiveness
- generosity, and
- courage.

I chose these particular virtues because they are the ones people mentioned to me most often in connection with their work – both the challenges of living them, and the ideal of living them on a daily basis. What began as a service to men and women in business gradually attracted the interest of people in other professions. It is my desire that in these pages you will find guidance in the experience of others, hope for your work-faith journey, and encouragement to live a blessed life.

Blessed are those who seek for wisdom;
for they shall judge wisely

Ultimately we do not thirst for fame or fortune,
comfort and security, but for meaning.
We want our lives to matter.
—*Joseph F. Nassal*

There comes a time in the life of a reflective person when he or she starts asking existential questions such as these:

- What is the purpose of my life?
- Is my work contributing to the common good of society?
- Where is God in my life?
- What is the ultimate meaning of my life?

These questions seek not just intellectual answers but wisdom. The learned eleventh-century theologian Anselm described wisdom as "faith seeking understanding." A modern way of expressing this idea might be "faith seeking relevance."

To grasp the significance of wisdom and its relationship to the workplace, let us take a look at this virtue from an historical perspective.[4]

The Book of Proverbs, a biblical source that is often quoted in business prayer breakfast gatherings, gives us the foundation of wisdom: "The fear of the Lord is the beginning of wisdom ..." (9:10). This is not fear in the sense of possible punishment, but reverential fear of the creature in relation to the Creator. Here, too, is the true basis of humility: "... fear of the Lord is wisdom and culture; loyal humility is his delight" (Sirach 1:24, New American Bible [NAB]).

In the Egyptian, Babylonian, and other early cultures, wisdom was looked upon as something distinctly practical, encompassing both moral value and good sense. The wise person was one who knew the principles of right living and conducted his or her life accordingly, in both speech and action. In Greek philosophy, Socrates, Plato, and Aristotle gave wisdom its speculative connotation. Wisdom was thought to be knowledge of self and the meaning of life. Tom Morris, in his insightful book *If Aristotle Ran General Motors*, explains one of Aristotle's primary discoveries:

> When he looked around at the world, Aristotle saw, as all of us do, that human beings pursue different things. Some seek wealth. Others dream of fame. Some long for love. Others lust for power. The cautious aim for security, the bold for adventure. But Aristotle had the insight that beneath all the surface differences in what we seem to chase, everyone in this life is really after the same thing: happiness.[5]

The Hebrew Scriptures (Old Testament) look upon wisdom in two ways: as something essentially rational and practical, seen in maxims or proverbs of conduct, and as a gift from God bestowed on human beings by a special grace. The practical application affected both men and women. The lessons in the Book of Proverbs and the Book of Sirach (Ecclesiasticus in some bibles) draw attention to the importance of the activity of daily life. Wisdom is gained by counsel and instruction from those who are wise. The wise person learns from mistakes by accepting correction, which is another aspect of humility. Wisdom affects human conduct in all situations, especially in morality. One is expected to display wisdom no matter what one's calling: merchant, administrator, judge, king, spouse, or parent. As

John McKenzie points out, "Life is unity and integrity which must be preserved from the dis-integration of folly."[6] Folly is the opposite of wisdom.

Israelite wisdom was modified by its relationship with God, whose wisdom is evident in creation. Wisdom is seen ultimately as a gift from God, who grants it to people. We see this in a special way in the person of King Solomon, whose wise judgment enabled him to make decisions on some thorny matters. For example, in the case of the two women who each claimed to be the mother of the same baby, his wisdom revealed the true mother and saved the baby. He showed such sagacity that all Israel "stood in awe of the king, because they perceived that the wisdom of God was in him, to execute justice" (1 Kings 3:28). In this sense, wisdom is both a moral as well as a practical way of life.

Wisdom is personified as feminine in the Hebrew Scriptures: "Happy [blessed] are those who find wisdom, and those who get understanding, for her income is better than silver, and her revenue better than gold" (Proverbs 3:13-14). She is born of God before creation (Proverbs 8:22-31); for those who find her, she leads to life and favour from the Lord (Proverbs 8:35); she gives a spirit of understanding to those who seek her (Sirach 39:6); and to conscientiously observe her laws leads to incorruptibility (Wisdom 6:18-19; see also 7:25–8:1). Her opposite, referred to as "Dame Folly," is depicted as being fickle, senseless, and ignorant, leading one astray from right conduct (Proverbs 9:13-18). Folly is the root of failure and will never lead to success.

The Israelite understanding of wisdom, then, is based on the reverential fear of God. Flowing from this relationship is its connection to human conduct, especially as seen in what is known as the Golden Rule. Because of the Covenant with God, one has responsibilities not only to God but also to others. The Golden Rule is the most universal guide human beings have for their ethical journey; it is found in one form or another in all the major cultures and religions. Here is a sampling:

Judaism – "What is hateful to you, do not do to your fellow man." (Talmud, Shabbat 31a)

Christianity – "In everything do to others as you would have them do to you; for this is the law and the prophets." (Matthew 7:12)

Islam – "Let none of you treat his brother (or sister) in a way he himself would not like to be treated … No one of you is a believer until he loves for his neighbour what he loves for himself." (The Prophet Mohammed, 13th of the 40 Hadiths of Nawawi)

Hinduism – "This is the sum of duty; do naught unto others what you would have them do unto you." (Mahabharata 5:1517)

Buddhism – "Seek for others the happiness you desire for yourself … Hurt not others with that which pains you." (Udana-varga 5, 1)

Aboriginal – "You must always remember that the two-leggeds and all the other peoples who stand upon this earth are sacred and should be treated as such." (White Buffalo Calf Woman)

Baha'i Faith – "Lay not on any soul a load that you would not wish to be laid upon you, and desire not for anyone the things you would not desire for yourself." (Baha'u'llah, Gleanings)

Confucianism – "One word which sums up the basis of all good conduct: loving kindness. Do not do to others what you do not want done to yourself." (Confucius, Analects 15:23)

Sikhism – "I am a stranger to no one; and no one is a stranger to me. Indeed, I am a friend to all." (Guru Granth Sahib, page 1299)

Taoism – "Regard your neighbour's gain as your own gain and your neighbour's loss as your own loss." (Lao T'zu, *T'ai Shang Kan Ying P'ien*, 213–218)[7]

Remarking on the Golden Rule, Huston Smith, a renowned professor of the history of religions, once said, "If we take the world's enduring religions at their best, we discover the distilled wisdom of the human race."[8]

Becoming a Wise Person

Becoming wise is a lifelong project, because circumstances are always changing. How to act in a moral way or judge wisely or counsel another in a wise manner continually challenges us. However, we can cultivate certain dispositions to be receptive to wisdom. The first is *humility*. King Solomon is a model for us of this virtue.

As he succeeded his father, David, and became king of Israel, he realized the enormous responsibility ahead of him. And so in humility he asked God for an *understanding heart* and an *understanding mind* to be able to lead the people and to distinguish right from wrong (1 Kings 3:7-9). In the Book of Wisdom, he writes,

> I too am a mortal man, the same as all the rest ... Therefore I prayed, and prudence was given me; I pleaded and the spirit of Wisdom came to me. (7:1a, 7, NAB)

The second disposition we need is *openness* – an open spirit to receive instruction from wise mentors and to learn from our experiences. An integral part of the spirituality of St. Ignatius of Loyola (the founder of the Society of Jesus, or Jesuits) is "finding God in all things," that is, in the ordinary everyday activities of life. To achieve this spiritual practice, we need to be open in mind, heart, and spirit, receptive to discovering the presence of God in our life.

The third disposition is *docility*. We need to be teachable. Docility is linked to humility here, to a recognition that we don't have all the answers and need help.

Fourth, we need to *know when human wisdom has reached its limits*. An insightful story that illustrates this disposition comes from the life of one of Israel's greatest sages, Rabbi Akiva.

> Three Rabbis were faced with the problem of the meaning of suffering. The first Rabbi, a very learned man, studied the issue long and hard, convinced that he could solve the mystery: he went crazy instead. The second, also learned in the Law, devoted many hours to uncover the secret: he committed suicide out of despair at not finding the answer. But Rabbi Akiva, when faced with the problem, realized that it was beyond his ability as a human being to understand the meaning of suffering; as a result of his decision, he was at peace.[9]

Wisdom as Divine Gift

Wisdom has to do with making good judgments, judgments that benefit not only ourselves and our families, but also the whole community. As a way to help men and women in business draw closer to God, the fountain of Wisdom, I designed a retreat for busy people. This individually directed six-day retreat is one that a person makes while continuing to go to work; for this reason, I call the experience a "Commuter Retreat."

The retreatant (the person making the retreat) would meet me at the parish where I lived, which was close to the downtown core, for one hour a day for six days. He or she would set the time. We usually began on a Monday and ended the following Saturday. To prepare for our first meeting, I would e-mail the retreatant some questions for reflection one week in advance. Responses to the questions – sent by e-mail ahead of time or brought to our first meeting – help me to know about the person's spiritual disposition and ethical issues. Here are the questions:

- What are you seeking at this time of your life: personally, spiritually, professionally?
- What are your basic core, or faith, values? What are the challenges you face to living them, both in your work situation and in your personal life?
- What are the primary ethical issues you face in your profession, in your company? How do you deal with them?
- How do you pray? Whom do you pray to? When do you normally pray?
- Do you experience yourself as loved by God in a personal way? Please give some examples.

I would ask the retreatant to keep as many evenings as possible during the six days free of social engagements so they could pray for a least an hour before we met the next day. To aid them in this task, I gave them what some have called "spiritual homework" – meditations in the form of handouts. In addition, the last ten minutes of each of our sessions was spent in total silence. "Be still, and know that I am God" (Psalm 46:10) and "Speak [Lord], for your servant is listening" (1 Samuel 3:10) are two key biblical passages that teach the wisdom of silence. I would introduce the retreatant to what is known as centering prayer, since many are not familiar with this form of prayer. (See Appendix A for how to do this kind of prayer.)

One of my favourite stories of the efficacy of the prayer of listening in silence came from one of my retreatants. Here is his account, told in the third person:

Robert is the Chairman of the Board of a large oil and gas company. He was in his office one day when a friend of his who is the CEO of another company phoned to ask if he could come and see Robert to seek his advice on an important decision he had to make. Robert said, "Sure, come on over to my office."

His friend Steve is a very extroverted fellow with a dynamic personality. Steve arrived about 30 minutes after the phone call, eager to discuss the facts concerning his impending decision.

Now, that very week, Robert was making the Commuter Retreat. It was the fourth day. Being a reflective person by nature, he really liked the ten minutes of silence at the end of each session. When Steve arrived and got settled in Robert's office, Robert told him about the retreat and about the value he found in the ten minutes of quiet. He suggested they spend the first ten minutes of the meeting in total silence. This was a shock to Steve, but because he trusted Robert's judgment, he agreed.

Robert notified his secretary not to disturb them. Then the two friends sat in silence for ten minutes. In the Commuter Retreat, Robert had learned about centering prayer. The prayer involves saying a spiritual word, or short phrase, in rhythm with one's breathing in order to center oneself in the present moment. Robert had a centering word. Steve did not.

At the end of ten minutes, Robert broke the silence and prepared to listen to Steve's concerns. Steve looked at Robert with astonishment and said, "You won't believe this, but I got the answer for my decision during the ten minutes!" And, he added, "Now, tell me about this retreat you are making."

By being attentive to the moment, in silence, Steve was able to hear that "still, small voice within" and discover the wisdom he needed. Steve later made the retreat himself.

The purpose of any kind of spiritual retreat is to draw closer to God in a personal way, and to love one's neighbour as oneself. The role of the director is to listen to how the Spirit of God is moving in the retreatant's heart and give suggestions for prayer.

As a Jesuit, I am steeped in the spirituality of St. Ignatius of Loyola. His Spiritual Exercises (a classic retreat manual),[10] and other writings have had a great influence on the kinds of meditations I suggest. I also draw from my personal spiritual experiences and the experiences of other spiritual practitioners.

After listening to a retreatant's response to the preliminary questions sent via e-mail, I often suggest that he or she prayerfully reflect on the first meditation in the Spiritual Exercises – "Principle and Foundation." A modern version of this translation follows.

> The goal of our life is to live with God forever. God gave us life because God loves us. Our own response of love allows God's life to flow into us without limit.

> All the things in this world are gifts of God, presented to us so that we can know God more easily and make a return of love to him more readily.

> As a result, we appreciate and use all these gifts of God insofar as they help us develop as loving persons. But if any of these gifts become the center of our lives, they displace God and so hinder our growth towards our goal.[11]

It is easy to see what clutters our heart and stifles wisdom – egoism; an un-examined life; narrow, bottom-line thinking: profit as the only motive; an over-preoccupation with the material world, to the exclusion of the spiritual; addiction to work, at the expense of our family and our health; compartmentalization of our ethics; fear of rejection that can lead to compromising our principles; and so forth. St. Ignatius understood the human psyche, and so the Principle and Foundation concludes with a challenge:

> In everyday life, then, we must hold ourselves in balance before all of these created gifts insofar as we have a choice and are not bound by some obligation. We should not fix our desires on health or sickness, wealth or poverty, success or

failure, a long life or a short one. *For everything has the potential of calling forth in us a deeper response to our life in God.* Our only desire and our one choice should be this: I want and I choose what better leads to God's deepening his life in me.[12]

Holding ourselves in balance is challenging on many fronts: family-work, work-leisure, work-prayer, work-health. It takes the wisdom of discernment to find the right combination. My friend Barry says finding balance is one of life's greatest challenges: "It is the Achilles heel of life and requires dedication and persistence," he once told me.

I came across the following story from another friend, Warren, that illustrates the possibility of balancing the temporal and the spiritual in one's life:

A couple of us were having lunch at a popular hotel. Our waitress was slight of build, with impeccably groomed silver hair. On this particular occasion, the dining room was packed, and if any waitress ever had reason to be in a frenzy, she certainly did. But as she moved from table to table, she exuded not frenzy but an infectious peace and pleasantness. When she dropped by our table, I commented to her how happy she seemed in the midst of the noon-hour rush. "Oh, I am so glad you noticed," she replied. Then she took a moment to tell us the secret of her happiness. Every morning before leaving for work, she spends an hour in prayer about her job. She explained how during her prayer she visualizes each table at the restaurant, each guest she would be serving that day. And she prays that she might be able to care for them as if she were caring for God in person; that she could be a blessing to each. Her greatest concern is that the guests she serves will leave happier than when they arrived.[13]

Donna Schaper expresses the desire for balance in her work through the following prayer:

Bring me out of the house of bondage today,
O God, into the house of freedom.
Hear my thanks for the work of my hands,
and heart and mind.
Release me from the guilt I carry at not
doing enough and never being done. Bring me into the grace of
completeness in incompleteness.
Sabbath me, from time to time, even on the job.
In the name of the true God.
Amen.[14]

Wisdom in the New Testament

As a member of the Society of Jesus, I have a particular interest in wisdom as found in the life of Jesus. I am not as concerned with a theoretical knowledge as I am with an understanding flowing from a personal relationship with the Lord. As theologian Walter Burghardt put it so well: "... the faith that accepts propositions, that accepts the whole Christian creed, is inadequate without the faith that is a wholehearted, unreserved self-giving to the Christ who incarnates wisdom."[15] Knowing about Jesus as the wisdom of God, and knowing Jesus in a personal way, is brought out beautifully in the following story:

> After a large dinner at one of England's stately mansions, a famous actor entertained the guests with stunning Shakespearean readings. Then, as an encore, he offered to accept a request.
>
> A shy, grey-haired priest asked if he knew the Twenty-Third Psalm.
>
> The actor said, "Yes, I do, and I will give it on one condition: that when I am finished you recite the very same Psalm."
>
> The priest was a little embarrassed, but consented.
>
> The actor did a beautiful rendition ...

"My shepherd is the Lord, there is nothing I shall want ..." and on and on.

The guests applauded loudly when the actor was done. Then it was the priest's turn.

The priest got up and said the same words, but this time there was no applause, just a hushed silence and the beginning of a tear in some eyes.

The actor savoured the silence for a few moments and then stood up, and said: "Ladies and gentlemen, I hope you realize what happened here tonight. I knew the Psalm, but this man knows the Shepherd."[16]

In the Commuter Retreat, I teach two methods of prayer whose purpose is to help people get to know the Shepherd, Jesus Christ, as a real person. One method, called "Meditating on Scripture," can be used for any biblical passage. This prayer practice uses the mind as a way to get to the heart. If you are meditating on Jesus, choose a passage from one of the Gospels and read it slowly, savouring each word or phrase. When something strikes you – for example, you feel a new way of being with Jesus, or you get to know his personality in a new way, or you are moved to a realization of God's love for you or for another, or you feel inspired to do something good – this is the time to *pause* and *listen*. This is God speaking directly to you in the words of scripture, giving you the wisdom you need for your faith journey (see Appendix B).

In the second method, you use your imagination as the passageway to your heart. St. Ignatius called this prayer "Application of the Senses," for you want to engage, as much as possible, your five senses – look, listen, smell, taste, touch – as you contemplate a scene from Jesus' life. The prayer using your imagination consists of taking a scene from one of the Gospels and imagining yourself in the midst of what is happening. For example, you are there when Jesus is born in Bethlehem; at the wedding feast in Cana; with the disciples on the northern shore of Lake Galilee; when the leper approaches Jesus for healing; at the well where he encounters the Samaritan woman; at the cross with his mother, Mary Magdalene, and John the Beloved; and so forth. You are there, first as a spectator and then as one of the participants The purpose of this method of prayer is to get to know Jesus more intimately as a friend; to come to a better appreciation of his values, his concerns, his mind and heart; to grow more in love with him. You will thereby give yourself more completely to his mission, no matter what your state in life or your occupation. If you have a well-developed imagination, this kind of prayer can lead you to a personal encounter with the Lord. I introduce this kind of prayer to a retreatant by leading him or her in it during one of our sessions. The passages that I use most often are the call of the first disciples (Luke 5:1-11; John 1:35-39), the wedding at Cana (John 2:1-11), Jesus with the children (Mark 10:13-16), Jesus walks on the water (Mark 7:45-51), and the Last Supper (John 13:1-9). Note that these are scenes where Jesus is active. In the prayer using the imagination, the focus is not on the passages where he is giving a discourse, but where he is doing something. (See Appendix C for the steps involved in this kind of prayer.)

It is amazing to me how even people who have never made a retreat of any kind before relate to praying the Bible, and what a profound effect this kind of prayer can have on a person's life. Consider the following story from David, who is a married father of four and an administrator in a large oil and gas company. During the Commuter Retreat, his focus was frequently on Joseph, Mary's husband and Jesus' earthly father.

> On the third evening of the retreat, my sixteen-year-old son, who has been a challenge, called home to tell us he needed a ride after soccer practice. There had been a miscommunication; the ride he was supposed to have didn't materialize. I was annoyed, to say the least. The practice field is quite a

ways from our house. I was tired from a full day's work and my wife was still at the school where she is a teacher. So, it fell to me to go get him. Interestingly, I had just finished praying about St. Joseph and some of the qualities in his personality. As I drove to pick up my son, not totally sure of the location and getting more irritated by the minute, I began thinking about Joseph and the kind of father he was. This reflection quieted me down so by the time I got to the practice field, I was at peace.

David related this story to me the next day. I asked God for wisdom and came up with the following suggestion for his prayer for the following day: Luke 5:1-11, the call of the first disciples. (Remember that the retreatant makes a commitment to pray for an hour between our visits.) I always read the passage to the retreatant and make some comments to keep in mind for prayer. As I read the names of the three disciples mentioned in this passage from Luke – James, his brother John, and Simon – David stopped me. With an astonished look on his face, he said, "My sixteen-year-old son's name is Simon James!" Then he added, "My son is a lot like Simon Peter was – impetuous."

As it turned out, the retreat was mainly about David and his son and their relationship. It was about David learning to listen to the voice of the Holy Spirit in his heart and acting on it.

We hear a lot today about moral principles and values, about right standards of conduct in the workplace. To help people on the Commuter Retreat to explore this area, I often suggest a meditation called "Christ the King and His Call" found in the Spiritual Exercises of St. Ignatius. The appropriate biblical passages for this meditation are Mark 16:15 ("Go into all the whole world and proclaim the good news to the whole creation") and Matthew 28:20 ("And remember, I am with you always, to the end of the age"). The latter assures us that the power of the risen Christ will sustain us as we seek to further the kingdom of God on earth in all aspects of our life. With these two passages in mind, I ask the one making the retreat to consider four questions:

- What values move the world where you work?
- What standards does the world judge by?
- What are the primary values that Jesus taught and lived?
- Which values of Jesus do you find most appealing? most challenging?

Then I give the person a list of the main values we find in Jesus in the Gospels: *Integrity – Compassion – Humility – Obedience – Self-Sacrifice – Courage – Service – Honesty – Prayerfulness – Forgiveness – Faithfulness – Gratitude – Generosity.*

I suggest that in reflecting on the questions and Jesus' values, people ask him for the wisdom to better understand how to apply his values in their work situation and for the courage to more wholeheartedly buy into his value system. Author Irene Claremont de Castillejo gives us a window onto these values in the following reflection:

> Only a few achieve the colossal task of holding together, without being split asunder, the clarity of their vision alongside an ability to take their place in a materialistic world. They are the modern heroes.[17]

One retreatant, a businessman who works in the downtown core of his city, came away from this meditation on the call of Christ the King with a new perspective on the street people he sees on his way to work each day. He was considering the value of compassion and how Jesus was in the presence of the poor and afflicted of his time. The man realized that his "non-approach," which basically ignored the homeless person, was not consistent with his faith. He determined to follow the call of Christ more closely by treating each street person, to the best of his ability, as Jesus would.

The Anti-Wisdom of Jesus

It may seem strange to use the word "anti-wisdom" in relation to Jesus' teachings, but if we try to figure out his parables and endeavour to understand some of his wise sayings, the term fits. Theology professor Stephen Patterson rightly points out that wisdom requires a willingness to think deeply, to take time to reflect.

He writes, "The words of the sage are to be contemplated, pondered, and considered within the context of one's own life. They must be internalized."[18] But consider the following wisdom sayings of Jesus in terms of the rational mind:

> "...those who want to save their life will lose it, and those who lose their life for my sake, and for the sake of the gospel, will save it." (Mark: 8:35; Luke 17:33)

> "One who seeks only himself [herself] brings himself [herself] to ruin, whereas (the one) who brings himself [herself] to nought for me discovers who he [she] is." (Matthew 10:39, NAB)

> "... from anyone who takes away your coat do not withhold even your shirt. Give to everyone who begs from you; and if anyone takes away your goods, do not ask for them again." (Luke 6:29-30)

> "Love your enemies, do good to those who hate you, bless those who curse you, and pray for those who abuse you." (Luke 6:27, 35; Matthew 5:44)

> "Many who are first will be last, and the last will be first." (Mark 10:31; Luke 13:30; Matthew 20:16)

> "It is easier for a camel to go through the eye of a needle than for someone who is rich to enter the Kingdom of God." (Mark 10:25).

What do these words say to you? About your life? About your values?

These maxims of Jesus defy conventional wisdom. Some are downright unsettling. However, each contains a profound message. Sometimes Jesus gives encouragement in his response to a questioner, as in the last quote above. In the following two verses, the gospel writer says, "They [Jesus' disciples] were greatly astounded and said to one another, 'Then who can be saved?' Jesus looked at them and said, 'For mortals it is impossible, but not for God; for God all things are possible'" (Mark 10:26-27). In other words, if a person's ultimate focus is on God and not on the temporal security that money and possessions give, he or she will find salvation.

My own call to join the Jesuits 45 years ago was prompted by another one of Jesus' sayings: "What profit does a man show who gains the whole world and destroys himself in the process?" (Mark 8:36, NAB). I was in my early 20s, doing well in the company where I was working, with all kinds of favourable economic prospects, when I started reflecting on the message in this passage. Obviously, it had a tremendous impact on my life. Does it say anything special to you?

Jesus' anti-wisdom is foolishness to human ears. St. Paul recognized this fact. In his First Letter to the Corinthians (1:23-24), he writes about the wisdom and the folly of the cross: "... we proclaim Christ crucified, a stumbling block to Jews and foolishness to Gentiles, but to those who are called, both Jews and Greeks, Christ the power of God and the wisdom of God." And, of course, the cross is part and parcel of everyday life, whether in the workplace, at home, or in any other venue.

To be ethical consistently, to be a person of principle regardless of the environment we are in, to be a person of integrity and honesty, even at personal cost, is a demanding task. We need the wisdom of God and the courage that goes with it to live such a life.

Anti-wisdom, unconventional wisdom, certainly shows up in the Parables.

A man throws a banquet, but the guests don't show. So he fills his table with anyone he can round up from the streets and the alleys. He creates an open table, with company as mixed and diverse as life itself (Matthew 22:2-13). A farmer hires day labourers, some in the morning, some in the afternoon, and some near day's end – but he pays them all a full day's wage (Matthew 20:1-15). A shepherd loses a sheep and leaves his flocks standing in the wilderness to go and rescue it (Luke 15:4-7). A man sows and reaps, sows and reaps, so that at last he has stored away years of excess for the tough years ahead ... and then he dies (Luke 12:16b-21).[19]

In the parables of Jesus, all the assumptions of human life are held up for scrutiny and are found wanting; they disturb our world view and leave us struggling to reconcile them with what we know. But if we persist, by taking the time to reflect on their hidden message, we come to appreciate a surprisingly refreshing new way of living.[20] New paths to inner transformation are opened to us. As theologian Marcus Borg explains, this transformation is from life in the world of conventional wisdom to a life centred in God.

Wisdom in Practice

I have met many good people in my ministry to the business community. Now and then I meet someone who combines their ethical ideals with wisdom, integrity, and courage in such a way that others are inspired. Such a person is David Irvine. David is the president and CEO of an international consulting firm.[21] He is also an inspirational speaker. As a consultant, he facilitates leadership development workshops and corporate retreats. His focus, he explained to me, is to inspire and guide leaders to authentically connect with themselves and those they serve so that they might amplify their impact in the world.

His work is built on a simple premise: great leadership cannot be reduced to technique; it comes from the identity and the integrity of the leader. This, of course, involves making deep changes within so we can be capable of transforming others. We lead with the inner strength of who we are and with the wisdom we have acquired. An ethical challenge that often arises in his work is this: To what end am I helping leaders transform? In light of this question, he shared the following story with me.

> I was recently invited to engage in a leadership development project with a chemical company. This is a financially successful organization, but not a moral one. They do not consider the betterment of *all* their constituents in their strategic development planning. There are potential health hazards and environmental damage as a result of the company's directives. If I took the contract, my company would benefit financially in a significant way. Even though the work was alluring – it would also provide opportunities in other parts of the world – the risk to my own identity and integrity was too high. There was simply too much misalignment between my core values and the values of the company. Consequently, I declined to take the contract. The decision of what work to accept and what to walk away from presents a moral and ethical dilemma for me. Sometimes it involves weighing the commitment to support my family with the commitment to support my soul.
>
> Or, I might have to ask myself if a request is a higher call to try to change an unhealthy organization. I find I need the following three core virtues to help me make the right decision: *wisdom, integrity,* and *fortitude.*
>
> The first core virtue is *wisdom,* the one that directs all the others. Wisdom is good judgment. This virtue was critical in making the decision not to take the contract from the chemical company because it enabled me to make the right choice. I like what ethicist Rich Gula says about ethics: "We cannot do the right thing unless we first see correctly." Wisdom helps me to see correctly, that is, to discern what is of

highest importance. Wisdom calls me to step back, to *stop*, *look*, and *listen* to the inner voice of my conscience.

The second core virtue is *integrity*. Integrity is about being faithful to one's moral conscience. I find that while honesty is truthfulness to others, integrity is truth to myself; void of self-deception or rationalization. Integrity enables me to be consistent between what I say and what I do in different situations. This virtue helps me to pass the "mirror test" at the end of the day. I am able to look in the mirror and see that my self-respect is intact.

The third virtue is *fortitude*. This virtue enables me to do what is right despite how difficult that might be. I have learned that the right decisions in life are not usually the easy ones! Fortitude enables me to "do the difficult right instead of the easy wrong." Fortitude is the inner toughness that helps me to stand tall regardless of the hardship, disapproval of others, setback, inconvenience, or anguish that can come when making the right decision. This virtue helps me to remember that this too shall pass. Fortitude is what turns my intention into action. I have learned over the years that, my feelings are my feelings, my thoughts are my thoughts, but my actions are my life.

David's story clearly illustrates how people can live out the freedom of the Principle and Foundation of the Spiritual Exercises in relation to their occupation. This meditation calls for a heart free of attachments – for example, from money, power, or prestige – to be able to make right decisions. Thus we are able to use personal gifts and talents that help us and others become better persons. For everything has the potential of calling forth in us a deeper response to the wisdom of God.

As I mentioned earlier in this chapter, certain dispositions can help us be receptive to the gift of wisdom. Here, I would add three.

The first is a willingness to ask basic life questions, like the one that initiated David Irvine's story and like those stated at the beginning of this chapter.

Second, one needs a listening heart. A wonderful story that illustrates this point comes from Tom, an accountant.

> I can recall at least three times in my life when I've suddenly become fully awakened at precisely 3:16 a.m. with the thought of John 3:16 going through my mind ("For God so loved the world that he gave his only Son, so that everyone who believes in him may not perish but may have eternal life.").

> The first time it happened, I tried to dismiss it as a dream or processing a thought during REM sleep. You can see or experience something during the day and dream about it that night, but there hadn't been anything that day that would stimulate such a thought. I call these night-time experiences my "spiritual wake-up calls." I think of them whenever I feel disillusioned about an issue or event at work or anywhere else, and the recollection gives me peace.

The third disposition is an acknowledgement that each of us has responsibilities not only to God but to all that God has created, which includes nature as well as other human beings. Truly blessed are those who seek wisdom, then, with an open mind and an open heart.

Thomas Aquinas, a man of great intellect and wisdom, wrote, "Among all human pursuits, the pursuit of wisdom is more perfect, more noble, more useful, and more full of joy."[22] I don't know if Thomas had the workplace in mind when he chose the word "useful," but if he were alive today, I am positive he would emphasize the importance of wisdom for all aspects of our everyday life.

2

Blessed are those who act with integrity; they shall experience inner peace

He labours good on good to fix, and owes
To Virtue, every triumph he knows;
—Who if he rise to sanctions of command,
Rises by open means; and there will stand
On honourable terms, or else retire.
—*William Wordsworth*

The Parable of the Good Samaritan

The wisdom of God is expressed in many ways. As mentioned in Chapter 1, the parables of Jesus contain kernels of insight that can challenge our common perceptions. Such is the case in the Parable of the Good Samaritan. Recall the story: a Jewish man is on his way to the city of Jericho from Jerusalem. On his journey, he is set upon by thieves who rob him, beat him up, and leave him half-dead. Three people see him lying in the road; two, a priest and a Levite, pass by without stopping, while the third, a Samaritan, tends to the victim's needs, and helps him get back on his feet.

When I present weekend retreats on spirituality in the workplace, I often begin with this intriguing story, because the Samaritan is likely a merchant on his way from Jerusalem to Jericho to conduct a business transaction, as he has with him wine and oil. He has enough of these products to use some of them to attend to the man beaten by robbers.

It is important to consider the overall context of this parable to grasp its full meaning. First, the story Jesus tells is occasioned by a Jewish lawyer who knows that to inherit eternal life he is to love God with all his heart and his neighbour as himself. But wanting to justify himself, he asks Jesus, "Who is my neighbour?" (Luke 10:25-37) Second, to pious Jews in Jesus' time, the term "Samaritan" had negative connotations. The Samaritan people rejected the traditions and rules of the Jewish religious leaders. They denied the validity of the Jewish priesthood. And they refused to accept Jerusalem as the only legitimate location for the Temple. Samaritans were detested even more than pagans. Third, each of the characters in the story, but especially the Samaritan, the priest, and the Levite, represent not only a role but, more important, an *attitude*. For the priest and the Levite, both linked to Temple worship, touching the dying Jew would render them ritually unclean. The Samaritan not only acts with compassion, but goes beyond simple charity to provide for the man's recovery. He is the true observer of the Law, because he places love above all other considerations.

Reflecting on the parable, we might ask which of these three men did *the right thing*,

The most obvious virtues practised by the Samaritan are compassion and generosity. (We will explore compassion in Chapter 4, and generosity in Chapter 7.) However, there is another moral principle manifested in the story: integrity.

Integrity: Having a Sense of Self

Integrity, first of all, presupposes having a sense of oneself, of one's intrinsic worth. The Samaritan has a true sense of himself; he isn't concerned about what others do or do not do, or what someone else might think of his actions. His reaction to the man lying in the road is spontaneous and non-judgmental. As it says in Proverbs, "The integrity of the upright guides them" (11:3).

As we age and mature we grow in our sense of self. Allow me to share some of my own story to illustrate this point. I joined the Jesuit Order at the age of 24. In the Novitiate (a two-year probationary period prior to taking what is known as First Vows – vows of poverty, chastity, and obedience), I discovered that I had a poor self-image. I also realized that my self-worth greatly depended on what other people thought of me; I had inherited both my father's natural gift for sales and its corresponding need to be liked, to please others. Coupled with this was a strong fear of rejection. These three disabilities are a recipe for disaster as far as integrity is concerned, because this virtue involves being true to one's beliefs regardless of another's approval or disapproval.

What saved me was a gradual dawning in awareness of God's personal and unconditional love. This spiritual realization became the main focus of my prayer life for many years. I fed on such biblical passages as Isaiah 43:4 ("... you are precious in my eyes and honoured, and ... I love you"), Psalm 23 ("The Lord is My Shepherd"), and Psalm 139:14 (where the Psalmist gives thanks to God that he is "fearfully, wonderfully made"). In addition, one of the older priests at the Novitiate gave me a phrase to say whenever my self-image was attacked: "God loves me and nothing else matters."

I took each of the above scripture passages to heart, along with the mantra given to me by the older Jesuit, and gradually the love of God became the foundation of my identity. But this realization had to be tested, refined, in order to grow. Over the years, I have been given numerous opportunities to speak about my beliefs and to act on them even in at times hostile, or potentially hostile, situations. Each time I have stood my ground, despite my fears and needs I could feel an inner peace. And so, hand in hand, my self-confidence and spirit of integrity, each founded on the love of God, have deepened my sense of self. Our sense of self must be grounded in something – God, family, country, etc. – that is greater than our desires, needs, and fears if we are to be persons of integrity on a consistent basis. Otherwise, our need for approval, or our dislike of conflict, or some fear, such as of rejection, will take over our heart and will.

"Integrity" comes from the Latin word *integer*, which means wholeness, completeness. Some synonyms for integrity are authenticity, congruency, and moral uprightness. Antonyms are dualism, compartmentalization, fragmentation. Various phrases have been proposed to try to capture the essence of this core value: doing the right thing, a commitment to truth and virtue, following your moral compass, being consistent in your commitments (both personal and occupational), doing what you said you were going to do, having the courage of your convictions, having an undivided heart, "walking the talk," and so forth. As a virtuous trait, integrity is closely connected with reliability and trustworthiness. University business professor Warren Bennis puts it this way: integrity is the basis of trust. When we keep commitments in a consistent way, we signal to others that we will do what we have promised to do and can be counted on to continue to do so.[23]

Confucius wrote this of integrity: "A superior person thinks of what is right. An inferior person thinks only of what is profitable."[24] Author Stephen Covey writes about growing in integrity: "As we make and keep commitments, even small ones, we begin to establish an inner integrity that gives us the awareness of self-control and the courage and strength to accept more of the responsibility for our own lives."[25] Sister Suzanne Noffke also points out the process of growing in this virtue: "As a personal quality, integrity in any degree demands the honest living out of whatever integrity has already been attained, which in turn leads to deeper and deeper integrity."[26] Michael Josephson highlights the significance of integrity for the soul of a person:

> We exercise integrity not to get what we want, but *to be* what we want. Integrity is not essentially about winning; it's about staying whole and being worthy of self-respect and the esteem of loved ones. It's about being honourable,

not as a success strategy, but a life choice. Though we may suffer for a time because of our moral courage, we will suffer far worse if we betray our own values.[27]

We each have certain heroes or heroines in our lifetime; one of mine is John Wooden, former college basketball coach at UCLA whose team won ten US national championships in twelve years. His view of being true to oneself is especially dear to me: "You must know who you are and be true to who you are if you are going to be who you can and should become. You must have the *courage* to be true to yourself."[28]

Integrity: Discerning, Acting, Saying Openly

In all of my research on integrity, I have found that Yale University professor Stephen Carter's definition best captures the dynamics of the virtue:

Integrity, as I will use the term, requires three steps:

1) *Discerning* what is right and what is wrong;

2) *Acting* on what you have discerned, even at personal cost; and

3) *Saying Openly* that you are acting on your understanding of right from wrong.[29]

Let us consider each of these steps more fully. Step 1 concerns moral reflectiveness, soul searching, and *discernment*. Discernment is hard work. It takes time and emotional energy. In our age, we seek immediate solutions. For some projects this is necessary; for decisions that have important ethical ramifications, however, speed is not a good procedure. Seeking a speedy solution leaves us open to the temptation to go along with the crowd or satisfy ourselves with the thought that "everyone is doing it." By taking the time to do the difficult work of discernment, we have a far better chance of staying the course in the face of criticism or opposition.

It is essential for Step 1 that we be in touch with our core values. This is so, as author David Lonsdale notes, because everyday life poses a continuous succession of choices between two paths: one leading to fullness of life based in the love of God, the other leading in a direction that is ultimately dehumanizing and destructive.[30] In the Book of Deuteronomy, God says, "See, I have set before you today life and prosperity, death and adversity ... Choose life" (30:15, 19). Our values and our principles, coupled with reason and conscience, enable us to take the necessary steps to distinguish right (life) from wrong (death). As Carter points out, not to reflect on the rightness or wrongness enhances the possibility for doing the wrong; we cannot know what the right decision is unless we think about it first.[31]

With this background on Step 1, consider the following life accounts of people taking the time to make sure they are following their values.

I first met Dominic on a flight from Denver to Calgary. At the time, I was just starting my ministry in the business community, and I had some anxieties about this change in focus. As we began talking about our occupations, I found myself telling him of this new endeavour and of some of my concerns. His reaction was very positive. In his enthusiasm for the project and his encouraging attitude, I received the courage I needed to continue. Since we both live in Calgary, we decided to continue this conversation over lunch. Dominic is a real estate appraiser. I asked him about the ethical challenges he faces in his work. This is what he told me:

> Within the daily course of my workday there are numerous decisions that I have to make. Most are made on autopilot and do not jeopardize my conscience. However, major decisions have the potential to be problematic. If a person has a steadfast core of morals, principles, and beliefs that he or she will not under any circumstances compromise, their possible problems will be mitigated.

As a real estate appraiser, I simply will not accept an assignment with a predetermined value conclusion that I must attain. If a potential client, whether it is an individual or a company, tells me they want the appraisal to come in at a certain amount, I explain to them that the market tells me what to appraise the property for. I will not, under any circumstance, massage the market data to arrive at an unrealistically high value. This is my "line in the sand" from which I will not deviate.

Case in point: a lady left me numerous messages that she needed an appraisal done on her house very quickly. She told me that she already had had an appraisal done that she felt was $50,000 less than she thought the property was worth. She also said she didn't care about market value. She offered to pay me double my normal fee to give her a quick appraisal at the value she wanted. I told her that I was not interested. Had I compromised my beliefs, I would not feel good about myself or my occupation.

One of the amazing things that happened soon after I began my Spirituality at Work ministry was an invitation to be a guest on CBC radio. An interviewer from the station had heard me speak about this new ministry in a sermon I had given at St. Mary's Cathedral in Calgary one Sunday. He phoned me the next day and asked if I would like to be on an early morning talk show, one that a lot of people in business listen to on their way to work. I gladly accepted. And so it was that the ministry got launched in a very public way.

Soon after I got home from the radio station, I received a phone call from a man who said he was calling me from his car cell phone; he had heard the interview and wanted to discuss some ethical issues he was dealing with. We met a week later for lunch. His name is Len and he is an architect. He explained that he had some serious concerns about the ethics of his industry. Our visit took place in early August 2002. At this time, a number of public corporate scandals were brewing on Wall Street and in Canada. At that time, Len was serving as President of the Alberta Association of Architects. I could tell by our conversation that he was struggling with the effects of some negative experiences he had had. He is a man of high ideals and was finding it difficult to reconcile these with some of the unethical behaviour he had witnessed. He also wondered aloud how he might make known his concerns to his colleagues in the Association. Upon some serious reflection and discernment, he decided to share his thoughts via the annual President's Message that is published in the Association's magazine. What he wrote and, in my opinion, shared with integrity and courage, follows here, in part:

> All of our professional associations throughout the country have a code of ethics. They usually form part of the governing regulations and by-laws that underpin the regulatory authority of the Association and are presumably one of the measures against which professional conduct is assessed should anyone step out of line in the course of their work. Why, then, are they often disregarded? Why are they viewed almost as the usual motherhood fluff that accompanies the eager idealism of a student or the entry requirements of the profession, only to be left behind in dealing with the "realities" of practice?

> With a number of company CEOs languishing in prison as associates muster the required bail, it seems that notions of integrity, fairness, honesty, and the public interest fall by the wayside in the pursuit of daily business. There seems to be a compartmentalization of thinking that isolates our values into discrete boxes that have different rules as one moves from one box to the other.

> Although the Enron, World Com, and Tyco examples might be in the extreme, the behaviours are troubling. Everything seems to be acceptable as long as there is a "win": the job is in the door and we can celebrate the victory. Meanwhile,

there are many examples of truth distorted, truth misrepre-
sented, and just outright untruths that litter the professional
landscape. If codes of ethics are nothing more than hollow
remarks made in the circumstance of registration, we have
no right to call ourselves professionals....

It is true that our business environment is extremely competitive. It is true that we all must pursue our living and
differentiate ourselves in ways that can attract attention and
secure work. But it is equally true that we can practise with
honesty and with integrity.[32]

Step 2 involves *acting* on what you have discerned, even
at personal cost. "Acting" means having the courage of your
convictions. In other words, it is not enough to have spent the
necessary time discerning the rightness or wrongness of an issue; you must do something with the results of your reflection.
"Personal cost" is an all-encompassing concept here. In the case
of the story of the Good Samaritan, the cost to him was his
time, the necessary oil and wine to clean the man's wounds,
and some of his finances to pay for the robbed man's stay at the
inn. For us, the cost can be minimal, tolerable, or drastic. On
the drastic side, there is the risk of losing our job by acting on
an ethical issue when the boss does not agree, which means a
loss of income. Our reputation may be at stake. We may lose
friends, or people we thought were friends, especially when we
take a stand on something controversial. Or, our *acting* may test
us emotionally.

When I was in my late 20s and still dealing with the tension
between my desire to be a person of integrity and my fear of
rejection, my emotions were tested in what for me was a very
profound way. I was living in an inner-city parish. I was not yet
a priest; I was doing pastoral work before going on to theology
studies and eventual ordination. We had a vibrant team at the
parish, made up of priests, sisters, and lay people; I was the
youngest on the staff. Sometimes at our weekly team meetings

we would deal with something controversial. This was the 1960s, the time of the civil rights movement in the United States, and the parish was in an African-American community. Occasionally, parish activities appeared in the newspapers, which made people in the bishop's office nervous.

One time, the bishop himself sent a letter to the pastor asking us to cease a particular activity. We were each given a copy of the letter a few days before a staff meeting, with the request to read it and comment on it at the meeting. The team usually sided with the pastor, who was a bit of a rebel, and, although he preached collegiality, had an autocratic personality. He reminded me of my father. I took the letter to my room and read it – and immediately wished I hadn't, because I agreed with the bishop. Fear rose up in me as I imagined myself being the only one disagreeing with the pastor and the rest of the team at the staff meeting. It was more than the fear of rejection this time; it was the fear of being seen as not belonging to the group. I took my concerns to God in prayer, and asked for the courage to say what I believed. I remembered a passage from the prophet Isaiah in which he reflects on his disposition for ministry: "Morning by morning [God] wakens – wakens my ear to listen as those who are taught … and I was not rebellious, I did not turn backward" (50:4-5). And in verse 7, "The Lord God helps me; therefore I have not been disgraced …." Thus fortified, I went to the meeting and acted out my discernment by speaking the truth as I understood it. Sure enough, I was the lone dissenting voice. But what a sense of inner freedom I felt as I left that meeting! I had risked all and gained even more.

Not all stories of acting even at personal cost, however, have a happy outcome. My friend George, who is now retired, told me the following story of a work experience he had shortly after completing college.

I went to work at a company that manufactured moldings, window sash, doors, and other custom millwork. They also bought ready-made doors for resale. My uncle was the sales manager. During the first year and a half, I worked inside the mill, loading and unloading freight cars. I was also to observe the other work being done and aid the various workmen as they needed. I have always liked working with wood, so this was an interesting time of my life. At the end of this probation time in the mill, I was assigned to the sales department. I was given a company car and an expense account. I had been travelling my territory for about six months when I was asked to do something I considered unethical.

Here is what happened. The company had a basement, a main floor and two upper floors. I had been on the third floor and was coming down the elevator to the main floor. The elevator stopped at the second floor.

When the elevator doors opened, I could see my uncle standing there holding one of the doors we bought from another manufacturer. He told me to take it to the sander and sand the Grade Stamp off the top of the edge of the door so it could be sold as a First Grade door. (The grade of the finished doors bought from the manufacturer was marked in ink along the top edge of the door: first, second, third. This one was graded either second or third). I had a hard time believing what I was being asked to do, and from my uncle, of all people. I told him I couldn't do it. His voice got louder as he said, "Everyone does these things!" I still refused. He ushered me into his office, intending to show me how to write up the order. Again, I said no. He became very angry, talking loudly, and told me, "You will have to resign!" I did not write a resignation letter. To my way of thinking, I had been fired.

Both my example and George's happened when we were young. Let's look at someone who took personal cost seriously as an adult. It needs to be said first, however, that not every action leads to a loss; if it did, we would probably never take such risks.

Author Robert Solomon has this to say about the importance of integrity: "Integrity is what endures through change and trauma. A sense of one's integrity is what allows us to navigate the treacherous waters of ethical dilemmas ...."[33]

Estelle is a waitress, and a good one. She relates the following incident:

> I got fired before the holidays. I was a waitress at a popular restaurant. It was hard work, but I enjoyed it. One night, management had me using toxic cleaning solutions where the chefs were preparing the food. I told the manager that this was very unsanitary and that no waitress should be handling chemicals and food at the same time. He fired me on the spot. I have no regrets. I knew they might fire me for standing up to them, but I felt I had to do what is right.

Step 3 is *saying openly* that you are acting on your understanding of right from wrong. Going public on why you made an important decision indicates that you are not ashamed of your values and of doing what you believe is right. Without sounding self-righteous, you are able to explain the principles behind the decision. You are not so concerned about what others might think of you, or how they may judge you, that you would hide your motives. Being open can be challenging. As Carter points out, Step 3 seems deceptively simple, but is often the hardest of the three: the person truly living an integral life must be willing to say that he or she is acting consistently with what he or she has decided is right.[34]

St. Paul's Second Letter to Timothy spells this dynamic out very clearly:

> ... I remind you to keep alive the gift that God gave you when I laid my hands on you. For the Spirit that God has given us does not make us timid; instead, his Spirit fills us with power, love, and self-control. Do not be ashamed, then, of witnessing for our Lord. (1:6-8)

We witness in the third step by a declaration of our core values, which at times can leave us somewhat vulnerable. Consider the following account that illustrates the challenge of living Step 3. Stephen is a 53-year-old husband and father of five children, three of whom are in college. For 29 years he has been a financial advisor for a variety of companies. In 2004, he found himself face to face with a serious ethical issue.

> I had been working on a contract basis for a well-established banking institution for six years. In this capacity, the bank would refer people to me and then I would advise them as to their estate planning needs. I have three questions that need to be satisfied if I am to take on a client:
>
> • Do I trust this person?
> • Do I respect this person?
> • Do I like this person?
>
> If the answer to any of these questions is "No," then I realize I cannot work with the person, because for me financial advising is not just about business, it's about relationships.
>
> My commitment to these three criteria was seriously challenged the day the company referred to me a medical doctor who is the owner of the main abortion clinic in the city where I live. I have a strong religious belief in the sanctity of life starting from conception. Therefore, as soon as I found this out about the doctor and his clinic, I knew I could not accept him as a client.
>
> In terms of my three criteria, I would not be able to respect him. However, this would be the first time I would be refusing a client the bank referred to me and I did not know what the reaction would be. It might affect my contract, I thought.

I talked this situation over with my wife when I got home from work that evening. We decided to wait and see how management would react to the refusal I was prepared to give them.

When the doctor and I met, one of the bank's representatives, the account manager, was also present, because the doctor was also his financial client. During this visit, I gave the doctor some clues about my beliefs, but I did not tell him directly why I couldn't help him. I did not want to sound self-righteous or harsh in my refusal. By the end of the meeting, though, I think the doctor understood why I said I couldn't be of help. The account manager, however, had no clue about what was going on; I think his thoughts were on snagging this wealthy account.

After the doctor had left the meeting room, the bank's man said to me, "So, what can we do here? Is this a good opportunity for the company?" I responded, "This is not a good one." I then explained my reason why – my moral objection to abortion – and that I could not bend my principles to accommodate the wishes of the bank. He didn't say much in return; I think he was in shock.

A couple of weeks later, the financial centre manager, the account manager's boss, asked me to come to his office. As far as I can recall, this is what was said at that meeting: "Stephen, do you feel you can just pick and choose among the potential clients we send you?"

I responded, "It is probably in the best interest of the company if I pick and choose when necessary because some associations will go nowhere."

He said in return, "You do not have a choice. We expect you to take whoever we give you. If you can't do that you aren't much use to us."

As I left his office, I knew that it was time to move on, because I now knew something like this situation could happen again. When I got home, I told my wife what had happened. Even though this meant some temporary financial insecurity, we both had faith that other opportunities would show themselves.

She completely supported my decision; I can't tell you how important her reaction was to me. We had both gone out on a huge limb for our principles and needed each other's support to see it through.

Stephen's story brings together all three of Carter's steps. He stopped to reflect on the kind of medical practice the doctor was engaged in; acted on his discernment by refusing the account, even though he was aware of the possible consequences; and explained why he could not take the doctor on as a client.

Moral Loneliness

Many of our ethical dilemmas are in the grey area of morality. As well, some options are morally better than others. When faced with two "goods," we need the gift of wisdom to decide which is the better good for this situation. Being steadfast in our commitment to our core values enables us to consistently choose the best good.

One aspect of personal cost in acting on what we have discerned as the right thing is what spiritual writer Ron Rolheiser calls "moral loneliness." This emotional state describes the times in our life when we are not blessed by the kind of supportive companion Stephen had in his wife in the story above. When we are without moral companionship, we feel the sting of being truly alone in facing a moral dilemma.

Rolheiser describes this experience of ethical isolation:

Inside each of us there is a moral centre, a place where all that is most precious to us is rooted. It is this centre we call our truest self. It is here we guard what is sacred to us and it is here we feel most violated when someone enters irreverently or doesn't properly honour what we hold there. It is here that we feel most vulnerable. It is this centre that keeps us from falling apart.[35]

Such was the case in my own life when I was asked to serve in a rural parish. My religious community was an eight-hour drive from where I was living. I was on my own. What had not been made clear to me before I went to the parish was that an inter-family rivalry threatened to tear the parish apart. Once I discovered the negative dynamic that was going on, I tried to intervene by listening to both sides. In an ideal situation, this approach would work. However, in this case, one of the families was incensed that I would listen to the other family's side of the story. They retaliated by doing their best to undermine me both as a person and in my role as pastor. It was a very trying time for me, emotionally and spiritually. What held me together was my faith: in myself and in the strengthening power of God. A passage in one of my favourite spiritual books clearly describes the state of my soul during this ordeal: "We are troubled and disturbed, yet nevertheless in our depths we have some unseen anchor that keeps us clinging to God."[36] That "unseen anchor" was my faith, the ultimate core value of my life.

In the article I quoted from above, Ron Rolheiser reminds us that in the Western world, we often find ourselves in a moral diaspora – not only in regards to ethics in the workplace, but in all areas of social life. More and more people, he writes, are finding that their faith and moral convictions are not always shared by their families, their friends, their colleagues, or even their spouse. Consider the following story by Jane. Jane works for an oil and gas company in Alberta, Canada. One aspect of her job is to liaise with First Nations people (Aboriginal Canadians). She is a very sensitive person, in tune with the pain that others experience; she tries her best to understand the world from another culture. The struggle comes when she finds herself caught in the middle between management and an Aboriginal community. Here is her story in her own words.

In Canada, the Crown (the government) owns most of the mineral rights. Outside the cities and towns in the province of Alberta are large areas of open land. If an oil or natural gas company wants to explore for oil and gas in a particular area, it bids at a Crown land sale to acquire the sub-surface rights. Whereas most of the mineral (sub-surface) rights in Alberta are owned by the government, the surface of the land is owned by farmers and ranchers and by Native Reserves (Reservations).

If one looks at a land map, it is clear where the Reserves are. On these Reserves, the First Nations people own the mineral rights, but Aboriginal people also have what is commonly referred to as Traditional Lands. When the treaties were signed between Canada and the various Aboriginal nations in the 1800s, the treaties usually had a feature in which the Native people released whatever ownership rights they might have held to the Traditional Lands in exchange for being granted title to a Reserve, while also retaining the right to carry on their traditional way of life: hunting, fishing, and gathering. This activity was historically carried on over large areas of land, far exceeding those granted to them on the Reserve. This practice continues today.

The crunch comes because the oil and gas business mind thinks in terms of square parcels of land, whereas First Nations people think in terms of historical, large, irregular areas of land. A problem arises when the oil or gas company wants to drill a well to access their sub-surface mineral rights, for which they paid the Crown a great deal of money, but have to haul their large drilling rigs over the same land that a First Nations community is using, let's say, for hunting. To complicate matters even more, there are not easily marked areas on a map to let the oil or gas company know which First Nation communities may be using the land! This is the case because the Crown has historically dragged its feet in recognizing Traditional Lands in the same way it has acknowledged Reserve boundaries.

To get clarity on who claims traditional use of land in a particular area, I phone the government before my company goes for the land, or I call colleagues in other companies to find out which Native Band they deal with in this area. Still, because there is no clear-cut, organized system indicating which First Nations groups are using which lands, there is plenty of possibility for conflict.

I want to feel like I am contributing to the betterment of the world through my work. I do feel I am making a difference when I interact with Aboriginal people on whose lands my company wishes to drill a well or already has one. In business terms, I want a "win-win" outcome, for both the company and the Native people. These desires hit a wall at times when I attempt to explain to senior management the importance of our relationship with a particular Reserve. The main interest of the company is how we can increase our profitability by cutting costs, etc. It is important for me to be able to communicate to senior management how a good relationship with the people of the Reserve may cost a bit extra, but ultimately, when handled properly, can benefit both the company and the Aboriginal group. Sometimes this means I get caught in the middle. At these times I feel like I am in a time warp, caught between two cultures: the corporate one and the Aboriginal one. I have to communicate on a business level with management and on a much more personal level with the Aboriginal community. I have to be "bi-cultural," so to speak – able to talk in terms of profit and loss with management, while at the same time maintaining a genuine interest in the customs and way of life of the First

Nations people. This means forming relationships, not just business contracts.

I first met Jane at a seminar on ethics that I give to people who have a job similar to hers. She shared some of her struggles at the seminar, and I was impressed by her integrity and her compassion. Because of the ethical tension she experiences in her work, she joined a small intentional faith-sharing group. It is in this open and supportive environment that she can share her concerns and get the encouragement she needs to continue her "bi-cultural" role. This kind of group can be an excellent resource for people who experience ethical isolation in their occupation.

There are a number of ways for people to keep their integrity intact when faced with a difficult moral predicament. Bringing my issues to God in prayer for guidance and strength was the primary way for me in my rural ordeal. A friend of mine in the Calgary business community told me that recently he was faced with a difficult interpersonal situation at work that demanded serious reflection and a great deal of compassion on his part. Because of the Commuter Retreat, which he had made just a few weeks before, he told me, "I went beyond my usual 'I can handle this problem on my own,' to asking God for help, a help I received. The outcome was so much better than I thought it could be."

People of faith also need to seek out morally minded men and women with whom they can openly and freely discuss their issues. One CEO told me that it's important to think outside the box when seeking a mentor, for example, by finding someone outside your field who can give you a more expansive way of looking at an issue and keep you from being one-dimensional.

A friend of mine who is a mechanical engineer and the CEO of his company shared with me another source of inspiration when he experienced aloneness in doing what is right.

In my business experience, there have been a few times when I found it difficult to follow my heart on an issue because I thought I might be considered weird or strange until I heard about a colleague who had done just what I found hard to do. Seeing someone else make a choice with integrity and courage helped me to rise above my fear of rejection. It helped me realize that I wasn't the only one on the planet with these values.

3

Blessed are those who act honestly; they will be trusted by others

All deeds are right in the sight of the doer,
but the Lord weighs the heart.
—*Proverbs 21:2*

The 1990s and first decade of the new millennium saw some major companies, notably Enron and Arthur Anderson, go belly up due to corporate malfeasance. Other companies were bled by their chief executives for personal gain. It is a matter of record that this was the case at Adlephia, by its founder John Rigas and his son Timothy. People who were once admired in the corporate world – Bernie Ebbers of World Com, Jeff Skilling of Enron, Sam Waksal of ImClone, and Martin Grass of Rite-Aid – now are infamous convicted felons. Also in the disgrace column are Conrad Black of Hollinger, Frank Dunn of Nortel, and Sheldon Zelitt of Visual Labs. More recently, Bernard Madoff pulled off the largest investment scam in history, and Marc Dreier was charged with cheating hedge funds out of more than $100 million.

The kinds of crimes these men perpetrated are not trivial: cooking the books, insider trading, bribery, distortion of earnings reports, falsifying records, forgery, misappropriation of company funds, lying to government officials, and looting a company, to name some of the most egregious.

What lies behind this kind of moral failure? One can point to greed, as seen in the huge fees and profits reaped; to vanity in the lavish lifestyle practised by some of the convicted; to arrogance at the total disregard of those who were being financially hurt by the callous acts of those in power; surely to bad judgment, at the least, in the drive to win at all costs.

My friend Jacie, the wife of a retired executive in the lumber industry, told me that she thinks ego and competitive winning at all costs distract people from experiencing the essence of honesty and integrity, which are the soul's energy.

As one sordid story after another appeared in the newspapers, I started asking some of the business people I had met what they thought was behind the "value destruction" we were witnessing. One man, an investment advisor, shared the following:

> There is the fear of losing face or reputation. When times are great, senior executives receive accolades from multiple constituents – colleagues, board of directors, employees, shareholders, the media, friends, and family. However, when times are bleak, this can be a very lonely experience; they see the effect of downturns on their peers, and avoid at all costs having to face the music themselves.

So, add pride to the list of corporate vices. Another man reflected on the actions of John Rigas and his son Timothy: "I believe that they knew full well what they were doing was morally wrong, but they acted out of a lust for power and wealth, and then lied to cover up their actions."

Sin and Salvation

In religious terms, in the Christian community, ethical failures are called sins. Basically, to know what is right and not to do it is sin.[37] One of the meditations I sometimes give a person making the Commuter Retreat is called "Sin and Salvation." On the handout, I define sin as a rupturing of the proper relationship between myself and God, between myself and those whom God gives me to love, and to my own self by a life of inauthenticity. I ask retreatants to reflect on their experiences of personal sin in the context of God's faithful and merciful love. I encourage them to consider the dynamics in their personality that underlie their sins, with the suggestion that they ask God for the courage to name their moral failures, be they at home, at work, or in any other situation. Only by understanding this impulse to do the wrong thing and by having total self-knowledge (our strengths and our weaknesses) can we hope to change our ways.

A variety of words in the Bible describe humanity's tendency towards the moral negative – deviation, abomination, deceit, distortion, corruption, to name a few. In the Book of Proverbs, the word "folly" refers to the root of ethical failure: a fool is one who deliberately releases a harmful influence on others (see Proverbs 9:13-18).

One of the businessmen who answered my query about the cause of dishonesty in the workplace linked his reflections to a person's spiritual life. This recently retired auto and truck retailer in the United States gave the following example:

> My direct experience with unethical behaviour came in the late 1980s and early 1990s. The banking system in the state where I live had collapsed due to the over-evaluation of real estate. It was a time when key people in the banking industry did not resist the temptation of taking advantage of this inflationary manipulation. Their keen knowledge of cycles and monetary value gave them the advantage of selling their stocks while leaving the general economy and those in the middle of it holding the bag. It must be stated that not all in the banking business did this, but it only takes a few to soil an entire industry. Those of us who were playing by the rules, whether in banking or in my position as a car and truck retailer, were left to pick up the pieces. During this time I learned a lot about what motivates people who prey economically on others. It seems to me that those

who seemingly have no consideration for the public welfare and are only interested in personal gain are cut off from any knowledge of God and God's laws.

Each of God's laws is set into motion and works in a most exacting way. Here, I refer to the "Law of Reciprocal Action": what a man sows, so shall he reap. Every action is paid for in full measure, be it good or ill.

Obviously, not all ethical lapses are as gross as the ones mentioned so far in this chapter. We are each subject to temptations, though, and we need all the help we can get not to fall into them. In light of this reality, let us consider moral challenges and transgressions from a wider perspective.

Author Cynthia Heald expands on the notion of sin in her book *Becoming a Woman of Excellence*: "Sin — whatever weakens your reason, impairs the tenderness of your conscience, obscures your sense of God, or takes off the relish of spiritual things."[38]

Margaret, a business and finance manager for a branch of the US military, says,

> I believe the lack of a sense of responsibility to others to be just in all matters and to be ethical even if no one is looking is prevalent in society today. If you asked people if not working a full day yet being paid for it, using work time for personal business, even taking pencils home from your workplace affects others, the answer would most likely be, "No." Our society has stressed independence and looking out for Number One so much that many have lost the realization that we are all connected.

In light of both the individual and social nature of human beings, I would like to share a valuable tool for living more deeply an ethically honest life.

Stages of Moral Development

When I began preparing to present seminars on ethics to companies and business associations in 2003, I came across a reference to Lawrence Kohlberg. Kohlberg was for many years a professor at Harvard University. He started as a developmental psychologist and then moved to the field of moral education. His theory of moral development is based on research that human beings develop philosophically and psychologically in a progressive fashion – that we progress in our moral reasoning. Kohlberg has influenced a whole generation of teachers and counsellors and remains one of the key figures for educators in the United Kingdom and North America.

He identified six stages in moral reasoning. Moral development begins in childhood, advances in stages (ideally), and provides the basis for decisions about right and wrong over a lifetime. He believed that most moral development occurs through social interaction. Only males were used in his research; enter Carol Gilligan. In her popular book *In a Different Voice: Psychological Theory and Women's Development,* she adds the female perspective. Her research led her to explore how girls and women grow in their sense of morality. Whereas Kohlberg's view focuses on a "morality of justice," Gilligan's focuses on a "morality of care."[39] The preponderance of evidence now is that both males and females reason based on justice *and* care, the goal being an integration of the two.

Nevertheless, Kohlberg's six stages are instructive; they draw out, in a psychological way, what Cynthia Heald is describing in a spiritual manner. These stages always create an interesting discussion in the ethics seminars I present. Each stage includes a question for reflection. (Note: people can get stuck at a particular stage, which affects their ethical decision-making. For example, a boss can be stuck in Stage One. I have found it common for people to be at more than one stage at the same time in their lives.) A summary of the six stages follows:

- Stage One – The "Infantile Phase." This is the stage of punishment and obedience, literal obedience to rules and authority (parents, teachers, other significant adult figures). The child is motivated solely by self-interest.

The Question: What can I get away with?"

- Stage Two – Also in the "Infantile Phase." What is right is following rules when it is to my immediate self-interest. The focus is less on avoiding punishment and more on maximizing personal gains. A decision is morally justified as long as it benefits me directly.

The Question: What's in it for me?

- Stage Three – Is characterized by an attitude which seeks to do what will gain the approval of others. There is an awareness of shared feelings, agreements, and expectations. On the positive side, this stage follows the Golden Rule, the precept that one should act toward others as one would want them to act toward oneself. Carol Gilligan's "morality of caring" is appropriate here.

The Question: How will this decision affect my relationships?

- Stage Four – At this stage, the person believes in following rules and laws both in letter and in spirit, because he or she understands that this behaviour will contribute most to the common good of society. Fairness is a key value in this stage.

The Question: How does this decision maintain fairness, order, and uphold both the letter and the spirit of the law?

- Stage Five – People at this stage accept obligations to others as a given, and tend to consider rules, laws, and dictates with a critical eye. They operate according to internal principles, not based on self-interest, fear of punishment, or rigid beliefs. They have a respect for the rights of others (and for creation).

The Question: What are my responsibilities to others and to society in this situation?

- Stage Six – This is the stage of universal ethical principles. A person who reaches this stage acts out of universal principles, of justice, of the dignity of the human person, and of equality. Persons are never means to an end. The reason for doing right is that, as a rational person, one has seen the validity of principles and has become committed to them. Stage Six places a high value on integrity and having the courage of one's convictions.

The Question: What do I believe is the truly right thing to do?

Kohlberg found that many adults function at Stages Three and Four. Stages Five and Six are the most morally developed individuals. I believe Carol Gilligan would name Stages Three and Six as the highest.

How might we look at the questions in each stage in light of the ethical temptations one can encounter in the workplace?

- *What can I get away with?* People in Stage One figure that if the probability of being caught doing something illegal or unethical is low, and the punishment is negligible, the act in question can't be that bad. Some examples: selling confidential information; stealing a colleague's or subordinate's ideas and claiming them as one's own; padding one's expense account; false advertising; falsifying a resumé.

- *What's in it for me?* Some examples: marketplace exchange of favours – "you scratch my back, I'll scratch yours," as long as it benefits me first; steal something tangible from the company I work for; accept a bribe; accept gifts or services from a client that would lead to the possibility of a conflict of interest; insider trading.

- *How will this decision affect my relationships?* The temptation here is to compromise my ethical values in order to keep my relationships amicable. Some examples: sharing information of a confidential nature about the company I work for with a friend from a different company, information that would benefit my friend; writing a positive performance evaluation on someone I like, even though their work performance is inadequate; compromising my values in a staff or team meeting by agreeing with the others on an issue that I have an ethical problem with in order to be liked or to keep the peace. Here is where the fear of rejection enters in, a fear that I will be disliked by those I admire, like, and respect if I say or do something they might not agree with. The greater this fear, the more likely people will compromise their integrity rather than risk jeopardizing the relationship(s). As stated in Chapter 2, integrity and a grounded sense of self are intimately connected, which helps us be true to our values regardless of the circumstances.

- *How does this decision maintain fairness, order, and uphold both the letter and the spirit of the law?* The temptation here, of course, is to make a swift decision about a complicated business matter without spending the appropriate amount of time discerning the rightness or wrongness in the situation, or to think that one has satisfied their moral obligations by simply sticking to the letter of the law.

- *What are my responsibilities to others and to society?* In this day and age, "others and society" is expanded to include the environment and the various threats to its integrity. Thus, one temptation for Stage Five is to cut corners on environmental issues in order to save money and increase profits. Here also would be temptations that affect the sustainability of the earth and its resources. "Others and society" also refers to the organization one works for.

Temptations here might refer to executive compensation. Given the salary of lower-paid employees in the company where one works, what multiple of that salary would be ethical/equitable for the CEO and other executives to receive? Or, in the amount of executive severance, an ethical question to ask in this context is this: Am I taking more than my contribution to the organization warrants? The amount of executive severance takes on particular moral meaning when the company is in financial difficulty and other employees are being asked at the same time to tighten their belts rather than receive their normal salary raise or a bonus.

- *What do I believe is the truly right thing to do?* Stage Six represents a highly ethical person. I believe the biggest temptation facing such a man or woman has to do with the way he or she communicates principled decisions. This is one way in which Carol Gilligan's insight on the morality of care comes in, as it involves the virtue of compassion, and compassion is needed for a principled person to deliver a message in a balanced way. Otherwise, the moral stance risks being seen as dictatorial or self-righteous.

My friend Heather Jamieson, an educator, pointed out to me that later in his life, Kohlberg came up with a seventh stage of moral development. This stage concerns the essence of our humanity. The question at this stage is this: *Why be moral at all?* This question goes to the meaningfulness of one's existence as a rational human being. Stage Seven occurs at the ontological level (the nature of being), which is deeper than the moral one. For the believer, it is "rendering to God that which is God's." The words of St. Thomas More come to mind here: he described himself as "The King's good servant, but God's first." Stage Seven involves ultimate moral maturity.

The Inner Struggle

Temptations against doing the right thing are something every human being faces. The question is, what do we do in the face of these temptations? St. Paul captured the inner struggle magnificently in his Letter to the Romans. He wrote,

> I do not understand my own actions. For I do not do what I want, but I do the very thing I hate ... I do not do the good I want, but the evil I do not want is what I do ... Wretched man that I am! Who will rescue me from this body of death? Thanks be to God through our Lord Jesus Christ! (7:15, 19, 24, 25)

In a courageous act of humility, he describes the struggle of all of us, while at the same time giving us a ray of hope. There is a way out of this inner chaos, he proclaims. It is Christ, who overcame all forms of death – physical and spiritual. We can go to him in prayer for the wisdom to see where the temptation lies and for the inner moral strength to resist.

Authors Robert Solomon and Kristine Hanson, in their book *It's Good Business*, list eleven indications that a person has done something unethical: they may

- lose sleep
- drink too much
- take drugs
- can't relax
- become irritable and suspicious
- don't enjoy things I usually enjoy
- fear getting caught
- can't look people in the eye
- feel embarrassed with friends and family
- get defensive and argumentative
- become unusually belligerent in stating opinions (politics, sports, etc.).[40]

The following French proverb indicates the opposite experience: There is no pillow so soft as a clear conscience.

"Two Wolves" is a short story that brings together the dynamic of the inner struggle in a stirring way.

A Cherokee elder was teaching his grandson about life.

"A fight is going on inside me," he said to the boy. "It is a terrible fight between two wolves. One is evil – he is envy, greed, arrogance, self-pity, resentment, inferiority, lies, false pride, and superiority. The other is good – he is joy, peace, love, humility, harmony, honesty, kindness, empathy, generosity, compassion, and faith. This same fight is going on inside you – and inside every other person, too."

The grandson thought about this for a minute and then asked his grandfather, "Which wolf will win?"

His grandfather replied simply, "The one you feed."

The Ethics of Being

Pastoral theologian Rich Gula points out that interiority gets expressed in behaviour; right actions come from good persons. Actions are always expressions of what is in a person's heart. He suggests that there are two dimensions to ethics: "the ethics of being" and "the ethics of doing." The ethics of being has to do with what is in a person's heart – values, virtues, principles, beliefs, spirituality. The ethics of doing has to do with a person's conduct – actions, behaviour, duties, obligations, responsibilities. The goal is integration of the two into consistent congruence. The important questions to ask in this paradigm are these: What is my *doing* doing to me physically, emotionally, spiritually? What sort of person am I? What sort of person am I becoming?[41]

In terms of acting honestly, there are many reasons for personal failures in this virtue. In addition to the high-profile people mentioned earlier in the chapter and their negative motivations – greed, vanity, arrogance, bad judgment, and pride – the ordinary, everyday stresses of family life might lead to ethical compromise. As one business friend of mine, who is both a husband and a father, shared with me, "It is the fear of not making the mortgage payment, not keeping food on the table for my growing family, and not having enough money to support my children through college ... that causes me to hesitate at times or even to go against what I know is right." These are, of course, legitimate concerns and need to be factored into how each of us reacts to unethical work situations.

Three other obstacles to living an integral life are *dualistic thinking*, one ethic for my personal life and one for my work life; *compartmentalization*, putting my ethics into psychological "boxes," one for my boss, another for my colleagues, another for our customers, etc.; and *rationalization* – self-deceptive explanations for my actions. Dualistic thinking shows up in the most interesting places. When former Canadian prime minister Jean Chrétien was challenged by Canada's Catholic bishops on a particular moral issue and its relationship with Church teaching, he responded, "When I am the prime minister of Canada, I am acting as a person responsible for the nation. The problem of my religion, I deal with it in other circumstances."[42] Author Tom Morris heard a man say it like this: "Hey, I wear one hat at the office and another hat at home." Morris's response was "Yes, but you wear them both on the same head."[43] The very existence of the third, rationalization, points to a basic flaw in the human psyche. In his insightful book on leadership, James Hunter notes that the renowned writer on the history of religions, Huston Smith, states that all of the world's great religions conclude that humanity's greatest problem since the beginning of time is its self-centred nature. Smith also notes that the great religions of the world teach how to overcome our selfish nature. Hunter himself writes, "Our purpose here as human beings is to grow toward psychological and spiritual maturity. This is what pleases God. Loving, serving, and extending ourselves for others forces us out of our self-centeredness ... Loving others forces us to grow up."[44]

After all is said and done, honesty is the best business policy because what comes with it is trust. Even in pragmatic terms, trust is essential. It goes to the kind of person I am – trustworthy.

The poet Ralph Waldo Emerson captures the essence of this chapter in the following reflection:

> Each man takes cares that his neighbour shall not cheat him. But a day comes when he begins to care that he does not cheat his neighbour. Then all goes well – He has changed his market-cart into a chariot of the sun.[45]

4

Blessed are those who show compassion;
they will receive understanding in return

Compassion is a wounding of the heart
which love extends to all without distinction.
—*John Ruusbroec*[46]

Company mission statements and codes of ethics are replete with such ideals as integrity, honesty, accountability, and professionalism, but rarely mention compassion. And yet there are many opportunities to practise this virtue in daily work life: when a co-worker is dealing with grief as a family member is dying; in the process of having to let an employee go; in the sensitivity needed to communicate with people of another culture, especially recent immigrants; in the transition period after a merger; in negotiating agreements; and, in relation to the environment, what might be called "ecological compassion."

The Basis of Compassion

What is compassion? Basically, it means "suffering with." The authors of a book entitled *Compassion* explain it this way: "compassion asks us to go where it hurts, to enter into places of pain, to share in brokenness, fear, confusion, and anguish."[47] We do so in order to deepen our understanding of another's suffering. And herein lies its challenge: how can something that involves emotional pain be good? How can participating in the suffering of others make us better people? Perhaps by looking at the opposites of compassion – indifference, cruelty, hard heartedness, insensitivity, and ruthlessness – we can find our answer.

Compassion is the opposite of cruelty; it helps to alleviate suffering in the other, and turns indifference into genuine caring. Compassion recognizes our social nature: that the good of each individual is necessarily related to the common good of all, that when one of us suffers, we all suffer, and when one of us rejoices, we all rejoice. Consider the following two situations, one of which involves a compassionate response and one that does not.

Jim is in middle management of an electrical power company. Here he reflects on something I wrote on balancing integrity with compassion:

> I have been searching for a workable definition of integrity for years and this is the best I have seen. I had to fire someone yesterday because of both fit and performance. It was difficult, but based on your guidance and explanation I feel that I truly did it with compassion, integrity, and respect for the person's dignity.

Geoffrey Colvin is a writer for *Fortune* magazine. In an article entitled "The *Other* Victims of Bernie Ebbers's Fraud," he considers the full extent to which one of history's greatest financial frauds affected the lives of people.

> Sympathy has focused on the thousands of World Com employees who lost not only jobs and medical insurance, but also 401(k) accounts invested heavily in company stock. Next in line for sympathy come the company's shareholders, including many pension funds, which lost billions.

> Much more [damage] followed once the fraud was revealed and World Com filed for bankruptcy. Many suppliers immediately stopped getting paid, which was bad for all and terrible for some – local carriers were no longer being paid

to complete World Com calls, yet it was illegal for those carriers not to complete them.[48]

In the first example, Jim has sincere concern for the well-being of his employee who is being fired. In the second example, not only did Bernie Ebbers fail in integrity, but his actions indicated a total disregard for the common good.

Compassion has a prominent place in both the Hebrew Scriptures (Old Testament) and the New Testament. For the Jewish believer and the Christian, the foundational passage for being a person of compassion is in the Book of Exodus. In Exodus 1:8-14, we read about the life of the early Israelites. They were living in slavery in Egypt, where they were cruelly oppressed. They cried out to God to free them. Into this situation came Moses (3:1-6). One day, while he was tending the flock of his father-in-law, he saw a bush that was on fire, but the flames were not consuming it. He decided to draw closer to the bush to get a better look at this incredible sight.

> When the Lord saw that [Moses] had turned aside to see, God called to him out of the bush, "Moses, Moses!" And he said, "Here I am." Then God said, "Come no closer! Remove the sandals from your feet, for the place on which you are standing is holy ground." He said further, "I am the God of your father, the God of Abraham, the God of Isaac, and the God of Jacob." And Moses hid his face, for he was afraid to look at God. (3:4-6)

This is the *call* of Moses. His immediate response reminds us of the beginning of wisdom, reverential fear of the Lord, which we explored in Chapter 1 of this book.

Then God said to Moses, "I have observed the misery of my people in Egypt; I have heard their cry on account of their taskmasters. Indeed, I know their sufferings..." (3:7).

Here is the biblical basis of our compassion: the response of our compassionate God to the plight of his people. God sees oppression and responds with genuine care. He hears the groanings of a troubled people and determines to do something about it. God continues his conversation with Moses: "And I have come down to deliver [the Israelites] from the Egyptians and to bring them up out of that land to a good and broad land, a land flowing with milk and honey..." (3:8).

As with the virtue of integrity, simply feeling compassionate is not enough. We must also act on those feelings.

In the Book of Psalms, the Lord is often described as being a God of mercy and compassion. Consider these examples.

- Even when the Israelite people were unfaithful to the Covenant, "God, being compassionate, forgave their iniquity and did not destroy them" (Psalm 78:38). Why? Because "he remembered that they were but flesh" (78:39). Ah! There's the compassion.
- In a time of distress, David prays for help. He does so with confidence because he believes that God is merciful and loving, "slow to anger and abounding in steadfast love" (86:15). One can easily add the words "and understanding" here, which is the basis of compassion.
- In one of his psalms of praise, David proclaims God's greatness: "The Lord is good to all, and his compassion is over all that he has made" (145:8-9).
- In Psalms 111 and 112, the author explains two truths: that the beginning of wisdom is reverential fear of the Lord, and that the wise person acts as God acts, with justice and kindness, especially towards the poor (see Psalm 112:5, 9). Happy is this person because he or she is in harmony with God's ways. This, of course, applies to both our personal and professional lives.

In what might be called "the business person's bible," the Book of Proverbs encourages ethical behaviour for much of human activity. Virtues such as integrity, prudence, honesty, humility, justice, and compassion are highlighted with wise sayings aimed at teaching the experienced and the inexperienced alike. In the case of compassion, special emphasis is placed on the poor of society (often referred to as orphans, widows and strangers).

- Happy are those who are kind to the poor. (Proverbs 14:21)
- Those who oppress the poor insult their Maker, but those who are kind to the needy honour him. (14:31)
- If you close your ear to the cry of the poor, you will cry out and not be heard. (21:13)
- Whoever is kind to the poor, lends to the Lord, and will be repaid in full. (19:17)[49]

In the New Testament, Jesus is the incarnation of God's compassion. He embodies the Father's concern for the poor. He interacts so often with the outcasts of his time – lepers, a blind beggar, a prostitute, people who were possessed, and others – that it seems he has a preference for their company. Regarding the basis of his compassion and care, the following reflection from the book *Compassion: A Reflection on the Christian Life* gives us valuable insight:

> It was out of compassion that Jesus' healing emerged. He did not cure to prove, to impress, or to convince. *His cures were the natural expression of his being our God...* The great mystery is not the cures, but the infinite compassion which is their source.[50]

Jesus teaches by word and example that one of the main characteristics of compassion is what might be called "having an accepting presence" – also known as unconditional love. Whether the other person is someone in our family who is suffering, a colleague at work who is in difficulty, or a street person we see on our way to work, the compassionate part of our self goes beyond our emotional resistance to pain and reaches out to the person in need. As spiritual writer Jean Vanier states, this kind of openness might necessitate a conversion.

Compassion is not a passing emotion. It is more than a gesture of tenderness without commitment. To be compassionate is to turn with an open heart towards those who are afflicted. It requires a heart which is understanding and full of goodness, which seeks ways of giving assistance and support.[51]

Conversion to Compassion

Turning "with an open heart" towards another is what conversion is all about. First, we might need to get past prejudice or fear or some other kind of blind spot to our mind and heart. In my life as a Jesuit, I recall three primary experiences of what I have learned to call "conversion to compassion." Here are two of them.[52]

The first of these conversions occurred in the United States before I was ordained a priest. The civil rights movement was in full swing. I volunteered to live and work in an African-American inner-city neighbourhood in San Francisco. Having grown up in a middle-class white community, I had not had a lot of contact with black people before. It wasn't long before I discovered some basic prejudices in myself. Fortunately, I had some very understanding mentors from the neighbourhood who helped me to face and deal with my misconceptions. I also gained valuable insight through books on the history of black people in the United States. The openness I gradually experienced guided me to an understanding of the African-American story that was revealing and profound. It led me in the direction of being an advocate for the rights of black people. My main involvement in the parish where I lived was to find job opportunities for African-American men who, for a variety of reasons, were unskilled and unemployed. Half the time I walked the neighbourhood introducing myself to men who were out of work; the other half I spent contacting personnel people in San Francisco businesses and in unions in order to arrange job interviews. My heart opened in compassion to the people through this ministry. Despite the tension that existed between black and white people in those days, I had what could only be described as a remarkable relationship with the black men I met. But the reason for this connection came as a total surprise. I grew up with a domineering father, leaving me with an inferiority complex. African-American men in the inner cities had a similar psychological characteristic, though theirs came from a domineering white culture. One day while I was at prayer, the similarity between our situations dawned on me – my weakness intimately connected me to theirs. Personal weaknesses are not easy to acknowledge, but they often link us in solidarity with others, as I discovered.

My second conversion to compassion was in some ways the most difficult of the three. I was living in a house with six other Jesuits. Three of us were priests, and four were in theology studies, which is the final step before ordination. We were a close-knit group with some basic values in common: we wanted to live a simple lifestyle, we wanted to live in an economically poor neighbourhood, we wanted our home to be open to others in a genuine gesture of hospitality, and we wanted to have the kind of community that prayed together and shared openly with one another. Like any group of people living under the same roof, we had our stressful moments as well as our joyful ones. We began this living situation the first of September, just as school was getting underway. By November, we had grown close, and some lifelong friendships had formed. The opportunity for a new conversion for me came the day after US Thanksgiving. All but two of our group were still visiting their families who lived in the area. One of the theology students and I were having leftover turkey for lunch, when suddenly he said, "I want to share something personal with you." I had come to like this guy a lot, so I said, "Sure, fire away." He then told me that he was homosexual. Outwardly, I remained calm and kept eating my lunch. However, I was stunned. And worried. How should I act in his presence, I wondered, now that I knew his sexual orientation? Should my behaviour towards him change? Should

I put some distance between us? I sought the advice of another member of the community who knew the situation.

He asked me, "What is your orientation?"

"Heterosexual," I said.

"Okay," he said, "it's simple. Just be yourself and let him be himself."

This sounded good, but I knew in my gut that I had some homophobic tendencies. So, the next chance I had, I approached my friend and asked him to be a kind of admonitor to me. In other words, I requested that he call me on any inappropriate behaviour, such as laughing at jokes about homosexuals. He agreed. He also recommended a book that would help me understand homosexuality and the fear of rejection that some gay people have when they decide to come out. This book helped me to understand that being homosexual was not just about sex, but about feelings of compassion, love, respect, and generosity.[53] As I got to know this man better, I came to appreciate him in a holistic way. Gradually, my fears diminished, then vanished.

In these two experiences – living in the African-American community and living in the same house with my friend who is homosexual – I learned four important lessons. First, no one is exempt from prejudice; it is simply part of the human psyche. We can encounter prejudice in the workplace, in a country club, at church, or on vacation in another country or culture. Second, this bias, this preconceived opinion that is not based on fact, is a form of moral blindness and can lead to all kinds of discrimination, intolerance, and downright hatred. Third, prejudice is a block to a person's heart, rendering him or her ineffective in having compassion for the other's circumstances. This can be especially detrimental in a work setting, where employees may come from different countries, cultures, customs, religions, and have different sexual orientations. Fourth, we can unlearn a prejudice. Our wrongful thinking and our emotional deficiencies can be transformed, as mine were.

To facilitate this dynamic of transformation, I often use a prayer method that I call "Conversion to Compassion." The process goes like this:

- First, I become aware of an inability to feel with another in their distress. This means I am willing to admit I may have a prejudice or some other barrier to my heart towards another person or a group of persons.
- Second, I bring this barrier or block to God for healing. I do so in any words I wish.
- Third, I then leave the healing in God's hands with complete trust in his power and in his desire that I be freed from any obstacle to loving another.

I have found this form of prayer to be very effective. It has enabled me to have the kind of accepting presence that Jesus lived and taught.

Compassion for Oneself

When we think about the virtue of compassion, our reference point is usually other people or the environment. Perhaps we seldom think of ourselves as the recipient of our compassion. Yet, if we cannot be concerned about our own needs, how can we truly care for others? Neglecting to care for ourselves inevitably leads to burnout.

St. Paul has an interesting reflection on the subject of giving in his Second Letter to the Corinthians: "The relief of others ought not to impoverish you" (8:13, NAB). He is referring to money, but I believe it relates to our time and energy as well.

Balance is the key here. Balance is about honouring personal boundaries, about being able to say "No" in order to truly say "Yes." It implies having self-respect and a healthy sense of self-worth. To illustrate this point, here is an excerpt from Megan LeBoutillier's personal "Bill of Rights":

I have the right to say "No".

I have the right to determine how and when people enter my space.

I have the right to my feelings.

I have the right to make choices in my life.

I have the right to make my own decisions.

I have the right to determine and prioritize my needs and desires.

I have the right to make mistakes and not be perfect.

I have the right to be in a nonabusive environment.[54]

Being compassionate with ourselves is one antidote to burnout, for it involves caring about our basic needs:

- for love: quality time with family and friends;
- for good health: eating properly and exercising; and
- for spiritual well-being: through prayer and other spiritual exercises.

Underlying the ability to live a balanced life is the issue of personal identity. I first faced this realization when I was in my mid-20s. As I mentioned in Chapter 2, it was in the early days of being a Jesuit that I realized I had a poor self-image. In order to compensate for my lack of self-worth, I had unconsciously filled this hole in my psyche with possessions and prestige. I had imagined myself to be worthwhile because of the sports car I owned, the important people I knew, the success I had in business, the lifestyle I led, and so forth. I had fallen into the trap of confusing identity with description. The car, the people, the business success, and my other material possessions existed on the level of description, not identity. My salvation came when I realized that God loves me unconditionally. This truth gradually took hold and became the foundation of my identity as a person.

Anyone can come to a similar awareness of his or her basic identity. An unexpected job loss, the challenge to stand up for what we believe in despite opposition, a serious illness, the "empty-nest" syndrome, retirement, or the death of a loved one can force us to take a serious look at what gives us ultimate stability.

Psalm 31 captures this fundamental relationship with God:

> Be a rock of refuge for me,
> a strong fortress to save me.
> You are indeed my rock and my fortress;
> For your name's sake lead me and guide me ...
> ... I trust in you, O Lord,
> I say, "You are my God.
> Let your face shine upon your servant;
> Save me in your steadfast love." (Psalm 31:2, 3-4, 14, 16)

To live a balanced life requires self-knowledge. "It is wisdom to know others, it is enlightenment to know one's self."[55] The motto inscribed on the temple of Apollo at Delphi in ancient Greece is "Know yourself." The great Greek philosopher Socrates expressed this truth in a memorable saying: "The unexamined life is not worth living." Of course, we can avoid growing in self-knowledge in a number of ways. We can overwork so we do not have time to reflect; we can fill the rest of the time with "noise": the car radio, television, or computer; or we can give into fear of what we might find out about ourselves. "Know yourself" implies getting in touch with our negative as well as our positive traits; we may not feel inclined to consider the former. However, if we do not explore the negative traits, we are doomed to keep repeating our mistakes. For example, if I have a tendency towards being a workaholic and, at the same time, shield myself from self-reflection, I will not be able to read the signs of burnout until it is too late.[56]

Self-knowledge also means self-acceptance and valuing ourselves at our proper worth. After all, humility is truth. I like this quote from the Book of Sirach: "My [child], with humility have self-esteem; prize yourself as you deserve. Who will acquit him who condemns himself? Who will honour [her] who discredits [herself]?" (10:27-28, NAB).

A healthy self-knowledge includes self-forgiveness, which is a way to be compassionate to ourselves; this might just be the most challenging aspect of self-acceptance. Often it is easier to forgive others than it is to forgive ourselves. In *How to Forgive Yourself and Others: Steps to Reconciliation*, Eamon Tobin suggests that "inner tapes" or "inner voices" may lie at the base of our difficulty; we unconsciously internalize these in our childhood. He writes,

> The presence of these tapes causes many of us to have a strong perfectionistic and rigid streak which is very intolerant of our own (and others') mistakes, imperfections, and sins.
>
> Often the "inner tape" will represent a parental figure who was very demanding of us – someone maybe long deceased but who is still very alive in our mental processes.[57]

These annoying "inner voices" are sometimes referred to as the "Inner Critic," the "Inner Adversary," or the "Inner Tyrant," Tobin explains. He continues,

> They are called *Critic* because they censure us so much. They are called *Adversary* because they are like an inner enemy. They are called *Tyrant* because they hold parts of our lives in bondage like a tyrant holds his people in bondage.[58]

One way we can view ourselves is through the spiritual lens of the Bible. Consider the following excerpt from a reflection by Dorothy Hulburt, which situates our self-image in both its positive and negative aspects through some of the main characters in the Gospels.

Who Am I?

I am the sheep that wandered off alone, hungry and afraid.
I am the younger son and I have squandered my inheritance.
I am the woman bleeding and I have been bleeding for a
long time.
I am the man with the withered hand and I can't do much
for anybody.
I am the man with demons inside of me, destroying my life.
I am the one the robbers beat and left defeated on the
road to Jericho.
I am a face in 5000, hungry, and Your disciples say they
can't help me.
I am in a sinking boat on a stormy sea and You are asleep.
I am sick and lying on a mat and I can't walk to You.
I am deaf and want to hear.
I am blind and want to see.[59]

For the Christian, these statements point towards Jesus the
Christ – healer, teacher, compassionate friend, merciful leader.

Finally, a prayer exercise I suggest to working people to
help them keep sight of the bigger picture of balance in their
lives is called "Examen of Consciousness," and comes from the
Spiritual Exercises of St. Ignatius of Loyola. This reflective
practice consists of four steps or "points" that I have adapted
for busy people:

1. Find a quiet place and there recall that you are in God's
presence. You may have to be creative in finding peace –
for example, your car, a nearby park, a church near where
you work, a special room where you live, or, as one fellow
discovered, your bathtub!

2. Give thanks to God for what has happened in your life
since your last Examen. Recall the enjoyable moments, the
people you associated with, the activities that occupied
your attention, and the unexpected kindnesses you received.

Pause over each and give thanks for each. If this is in the evening and you are feeling tired, you might want to ask the Holy Spirit to help you remember.

3. Again, slowly look back over the day (or since your last Examen), recalling those moments which were not pleasant, perhaps when you felt you were not at your best. What were the moods or the feelings underlying these times? Times when you lost your patience or your temper – at home or at work; lacked compassion for someone in your family or a co-worker or your boss; dropped the ball on an issue of integrity; harboured a resentment against someone; or engaged in harmful conversation behind someone's back. Consider these moments in the light of God's love and mercy for you, and express your sorrow in words of your own choosing.

4. Looking towards the next 24 hours, what graces (spiritual helps) do you wish to ask God for? Perhaps it is the freedom to spend more quality time with your family and friends, or the desire and willpower to take better care of your health by some form of exercise, or the discipline of taking some time for personal prayer. You may want to ask the Holy Spirit for wisdom in making an important decision, or for a greater sensitivity to someone where you work, especially for someone who tries your patience. Or you may wish to ask for greater courage to defend the rights of those you see being mistreated or to defend the environment if you feel it is being exploited for financial gain. Entrust yourself and the future to the Providence of God (as expressed in Psalms 23, 27, 56, 62, and 131).

It is helpful if you can give 10 to 15 minutes daily to this reflective exercise, perhaps at the end of the day. Cover all four steps, with the freedom to linger more on one step than another, as the Holy Spirit moves you. The biblical basis for this prayer exercise is in Psalm 139:23-24: "Search me, O God, and know my heart; test me, and know my thoughts. See if there is any wicked way in me, and lead me in the way everlasting."

Regarding the first step, or point, in the Examen (finding a place where you can reflect), some businesses have a non-denominational chapel or quiet room for employees to use. I visited a company in eastern Canada that has such a space on their premises. It's called an Inner Silence and Reflection Room and is accessible to all employees. Once a year, the company conducts a company-wide survey to determine if the room is serving people's needs. On the survey page is a definition of the room:

> Instrument or non-economic tool set aside for members of personnel who want to be alone for a while during work hours in an atmosphere of inner silence, relaxation, reflection and, if desired, meditation and silent prayer without affecting the efficiency of the operations of the department where the person works.[60]

Such a room would be an ideal place to do the Examen, or just to get away from the stresses of the job for a few moments, or pause before having to make an important decision – personal or professional.

One of my fondest memories in my ministry to business people is about a senior executive of an oil and natural gas company who needed some space away from his office to make an important decision. He had made the Commuter Retreat and found the ten minutes of silence at the end of each session particularly meaningful. One day, about three months after the retreat, I received a phone call from him.

"Father Max, what are you doing right now?" he asked me.

"Just doing some paper work in my office," I replied.

"Can I come over and see you for fifteen minutes?" he asked.

"Sure," I said.

He drove over to the Cathedral Office and I greeted him at the door. "I want to spend fifteen minutes of silence with you," he told me.

"Fine," I said.

We went to the parlour where I see retreatants, and there we sat in complete silence for the fifteen minutes. At the end of the time, he simply said thanks and left. He had found what he needed in this "sacred space."

Compassion for oneself is eloquently encouraged by Jesus in Matthew's Gospel: "Come to me, all you that are weary and are carrying heavy burdens, and I will give you rest. Take my yoke upon you, and learn from me; for I am gentle and humble in heart; and you will find rest for your souls" (11:28-29).

Compassion for Others in the Workplace

Let us return for a moment to the Parable of the Good Samaritan. We saw in Chapter 2 that the Samaritan in the story is likely a merchant on his way from Jerusalem to Jericho to conduct his business. On his journey, he sees a man lying in the road; robbers had beaten him, robbed him, and left him half dead. The merchant interrupts his schedule to attend to the man's wounds, pouring in oil and wine. He then hoists the injured man on his own beast and takes him to a nearby inn where he can receive additional care and have a place to recover. When I consider this story and the compassion shown to the man on the road, I think of something Mother Teresa used to say to the sisters who worked with her, "Love Jesus in all his distressing disguises."

Not all of our compassion for others involves people who are in such desperate need of help as the man in the Good Samaritan story, but as writer Bill Spohn put it, we must develop a "compassionate vision."[61]

In terms of ethical behaviour in the workplace, compassion means having a genuine concern for everyone in the organization, from the highest paid to the lowest paid. Here are some practical examples of how an organization might live out a compassionate vision:

- providing workplace health programs
- offering bereavement counselling
- promoting to supervisory positions men and women who have people skills and not just technical expertise
- providing training programs for people who come from another country or culture
- having a structure in place to ease merger transitions
- developing procedures for those who are being laid off (see below)
- making a corporate chaplain available to assist employees who are encountering difficulties in their lives
- engaging in what is known as "creative negotiating" (see below)
- staying alert and sensitive to the human consequences of business decisions
- remaining alert and conscientious regarding the effect of business practices on the environment (compassion for the earth).

In the matter of layoffs, the Tomasso Corporation of Montreal, Québec, a provider of quality frozen dinners and entrées, has impressive practices in place. Knowing that all companies have ups and downs that can lead to people being laid off, temporarily or permanently, the company faces this possibility with an attitude of fairness and kindness. A manager calls a person who was laid off three months earlier to say hello and get the latest news; a director invites several people who were laid off six months to a year earlier to meet for coffee and donuts or for a simple meal just to chat and actively recognize their human dignity.

These activities clearly flow from the company's mission statement, which reads in part, "to innovatively generate continuous growth … in human well-being, in customer enthusiasm, in long-term economic performance."[62]

In terms of negotiating, certain skills are essential to developing and maintaining productive working relationships. My ministry to business people has given me the opportunity to interact with men and women from a variety of industries. One of my activities has been presentating seminars on ethics to members of an association who are involved in negotiation on a daily basis. I am indebted to this organization for the following insights of William Taylor on "creative negotiating":

> People often view negotiating as a choice between "hard" and "soft" approaches. Basically, "hard" negotiation means seeing the conflict as a "zero sum game". If one person gains, it must be at the other's expense since the rules of this form of bargaining dictate that the sum of the gains and losses must always be zero; each side takes a firm position, attacking the other side while defending their own position.

> Not a good recipe for compassion as there is a high probability that the relationship will be damaged.

> In "soft" negotiating, one side makes concessions quickly, does not want to provoke the other side, and subverts their own interests, even yielding to threats if it means saving the relationship. This position does not serve compassion, either, because one side becomes a doormat for the other.

> However, there is a third alternative. It's called, "creative negotiating". The following principles form the creative negotiating approach:

> - the focus is on interests, not positions
> - there is a mutual search for creative options
> - the parties use objective standards
> - the approach is hard on the problem and soft on the people.

The interest in creative negotiating is that an agreement be reached that benefits both parties, a "Win-Win" solution. Both sides have their interests met. The relationship remains intact in the negotiating, or is improved, and the foundation is laid for successful future negotiations. With a focus on seeking to understand the other's point of view, this approach clearly is the more compassionate one.[63]

Compassion is often spoken of these days as a function of Emotional Intelligence. This form of knowing gives us our awareness of our own and other people's feelings. The more we develop this competency, the more we will be persons of empathy, able to relate to and work more effectively with others. Sometimes our efforts take the form of "tough love." Consider the following story from Chris, who has worked for many years in real estate development and management.

I was young, just out of college, when I went to work for a real estate developer. Working for Bill was a major eye-opener for me in many ways.

I was the office manager and so I saw Bill often and witnessed perhaps more of his behaviour than I was intended to see. Bill was a brilliant man from 9:00 a.m. to noon. He made decisions that involved some major development projects. However, from noon to 4:00 p.m., he was at a bar drinking with his buddies. When he returned to the office, his manner towards the staff was abusive, to say the least. I was especially sensitive to his behaviour because my mother also worked in the office. I vowed I would never drink during a workday, because I saw the effect alcohol had on the morale of the employees, myself included.

As manager I was concerned for the good of the company and its employees.

So, eventually, I decided to talk to Bill about his drinking. I enlisted the help of his wife, who was a friend of my mother and father's. Bill's wife was very willing to get involved because she loved the guy and they had children who were affected by his drinking. His wife and I decided to confront Bill about his problem. We did so one morning in his office.

First, we were able to convince him to get help for his addiction. Then we suggested he sell his assets in the company and pursue another interest of his: racehorses. The good news is that he did quit drinking and pursued other business interests, including the horses.

Chris exhibited compassion on a number of levels: for the employees, for Bill himself, and for Bill's family. And, as often happens, he learned from Bill's behaviour and its effects on the people closest to him how not to behave.

This story is an excellent illustration of what psychologist Carol Gilligan calls the "morality of care." (We discussed this idea in Chapter 3.) The morality of care, which emphasizes interconnectedness, is based on the premise that people have responsibilities towards others. In this understanding, morality is an imperative to care for others.

It is not unusual to find this form of morality in codes of ethics in the health field. For example, CHRISTUS Health, which has its headquarters in Dallas, Texas, subtitles its code of ethics "A Basis for Relationships." The code reads, in part,

> As CHRISTUS strives to fulfill its Mission and to live in accord with its Core Values, it wishes to be recognized as a community of service improving the health of the communities it serves. CHRISTUS seeks to provide effective, compassionate care, especially to persons who are poor and underserved.[64]

Speaking of codes of ethics, in order that they may be fully effective, the Institute of Business Ethics of London, UK, suggests twelve steps for implementing an effective code.

1. *Endorsement*: Make sure your code is endorsed by your chairman and CEO.

2. *Integration*: At the time it is issued, produce a strategy for integrating the code into the running of your business.

3. *Circulation*: Send the code to all staff in a readable and printable form and give to all new employees joining your company.

4. *Personal response*: Give all staff the opportunity to respond personally to the content of the code. An employee should know how to react if he or she is faced with a potential breach of the code or is in doubt about the course of action involving an ethical choice.

5. *Affirmation*: Have a procedure for managers and supervisors to regularly state that they and their staff understand and apply the provisions of the code and raise matters not covered by it.

6. *Contracts*: Consider making adherence to the code obligatory by including reference to it in all contracts of employment and linking it with disciplinary procedures.

7. *Regular review*: Have a procedure for regular review and updating of the code.

8. *Enforcement*: Employees and others should be fully aware of the consequences of breaching the code.

9. *Training*: Ask those responsible for company training programs at all levels to include issues raised by the code in their programs.

10. *Translation*: See that the code is translated for use in overseas subsidiaries or other places where English is not the principal language.

11. *Distribution*: Make copies of the code available to business partners (suppliers, customers, etc.) and expect their compliance.

12. *Annual report*: Reproduce or insert a copy of the code in your annual report so that shareholders and the wider

public know about your company's position on ethical matters.[65]

There is sensitivity in these steps – not only to a company's employees, but also to its stakeholders: suppliers, customers, and others.

Occasionally, we find the virtue of compassion in a business company's primary documents. Bechtel Engineering Corporation has what it calls "Leadership Covenants." There are nine such Covenants. Here are five of them.

- *Treat Bechtel colleagues with mutual respect, trust, and dignity* and believe they are acting in the best interest of the company.
- *Help each other;* ask for and give help and welcome it freely (it is not a sign of weakness). Go out of the way to provide extra support to fellow employees.
- *Communicate early, honestly, and completely* with all who have a direct interest in the subject. Listen to others' points of view.
- *Never undermine colleagues* directly or indirectly.
- *Work jointly to resolve disagreements* in good faith.

Mutual respect, providing extra support to fellow employees, listening to others' points of view, and working jointly to resolve disagreements are all manifestations of compassion.

EnCana, one of Canada's leading independent natural gas companies, has what it calls "Our Corporate Constitution." This document sets out the foundation of the company's values and is intended to be an "inner compass" that helps employees move in the right ethical direction. As it says on the company home page, "The Corporate Constitution sets out what we expect of one another; it inspires us, it empowers us; and it makes us accountable to one another."[66]

One would expect such a document to include values such as integrity and honesty as being important to the company's culture, and they are indeed found there. But there is also an equal emphasis on courtesy and respect. In regard to courtesy, the constitution states, "We communicate with courtesy, striving to treat others the way we would wish to be treated." This, of course, is the essence of the Golden Rule. Under respect, it states, "We show respect for the people, culture, laws, and traditions of the regions where we live and work." In Canada, where much of the company's work happens, an ongoing challenge is being sensitive to Aboriginal people and their culture. Efforts to understand and appreciate another culture are at the heart of having a "compassionate vision." This is true, of course, whether we are talking about a culture in one's own country or in a foreign country.

Lest compassion be no more than mere sentimentality, it needs to be balanced with accountability. The two go hand in hand, as John Beckett points out:

> In business, it is not enough that compassion and accountability simply be present. They must be in balance. The modern work world is characterized by imbalance, with the scales heavily tipped away from compassion toward accountability. A way to bring them into balance is found in the Golden Rule, which requires us to put ourselves in the shoes of the other person.[67]

My friend Leo is the director of a department in a large industrial company. In this job, he is responsible for 90 other employees. Here he shares the struggle he sometimes encounters in maintaining a balance between compassion and responsibility with those in his department.

> Our company has a very generous policy for people who need time off for stress leave or because they are seeking treatment for an addiction, such as alcoholism. While they are on leave, they receive full pay. When they are able to return we give them transition time: for example, we allow a lesser daily or weekly workload, and, if necessary, move

them to a new job, again at full salary and with medical benefits.

The situation I want to share concerns two people who report directly to me.

Both were on short-term disability leaves at the same time: one for four months due to treatment for an addiction, and the other for a five-month stress leave. We obviously hope that people in these circumstances will come back to work for us after their absence. The person who had been away for five months reported to me that during his stress leave he took his family on a three-week vacation to Europe. When he returned to work, he still wanted to have his annual six-week vacation. Not only that, but he wanted to take half of it during the Christmas holidays (which were just two months from when he came off the stress leave).

I felt this person was abusing the compassionate system of the company. In my opinion, he should have offered three of the six weeks back to the company to make up for the three-week vacation in Europe.

It is important to know that while a person is on leave, there will be some organizational change; someone has to pick up his or her workload. Plus, when the person returns to work, we may have to find them a new position in the company.

The person in question has been a good employee. However, my respect for him diminished due to what I perceive as a lack of loyalty on his part, both to the company and to his co-workers. I decided to share my thoughts with him on this matter. If I didn't, I knew it would be difficult for me to continue to treat him in a civil or even friendly manner.

After Leo shared this story with me, he explained further. "This is one of those everyday ethical issues that managers face. I am aware of the fact that compassion is one of the most challenging virtues to practise in the business world. It is not a virtue you hear much about. However, there has to be a balance between compassion and responsibility by employees, and a balance between integrity and compassion for a manager; without the latter he or she becomes an autocrat, without the former, a doormat."

Leo's understanding of the need to balance integrity and compassion has been an insight of my own, though in a different context. At the age of 33, shortly after I was ordained a priest, I was appointed by my Provincial Superior to be his assistant for what we call Social Ministries. One of my tasks was to visit various Jesuit institutions — high schools, universities, retreat houses, and parishes — and give talks to the Jesuits there on the integration of our spirituality (of St. Ignatius of Loyola) and social justice. This was in the early 1970s, when it wasn't very popular to speak on this issue, even among Jesuits. My deep-seated fear of rejection, the fear that I would lose the friendship of those people I most value if I took a stance on this unpopular issue, added to the challenge. The people I most admired, liked, and respected in 1972 were the Jesuits of my Province.

Two interesting dynamics emerged from the experience of this ministry. On the one hand, to be true to the mission the Provincial had given me and to my own integrity, I had to face the fear of rejection once again, which I was able to do with God's help. On the other hand, because my audience wasn't overly enthusiastic about the topic, I had to balance forthrightness with compassion. A passage from the Bible that was a great help for me in this endeavour comes from Isaiah:

> Here is my servant, whom I uphold,
> my chosen one in whom my soul delights;
> I have put my Spirit upon him
> he will bring forth justice to the nations.
> He will not cry or lift up his voice,
> or make it heard in the street;

a bruised reed he will not break,
and a dimly burning wick he will not quench,
he will faithfully bring forth justice.
(Isaiah 42:1-3)

I learned to interpret "a bruised reed" and "a dimly burning wick" as the sensitivities of my listeners as I presented what was for them a challenging and sometimes threatening message. As a result, many Jesuits told me they felt comfortable listening to my thoughts on social justice and Ignatian spirituality, because they found me to be low key and non-threatening.

Two Champions of Compassion

We have considered compassion in itself, as the virtue that "asks us to go where it hurts" in order to help alleviate the sufferings of others. We have reflected on the importance of having compassion for ourselves and the need for balance in our lives.

Then we turned our attention to some of the challenges of being compassionate to others, especially where we work, with some practical examples from the working world.

I would like to offer two final reflections. The first concerns being a consistently compassionate person regardless of the level of support from our companions. The second shocks us out of any complacency we might have in reaching out to those in need.

I am indebted to my friend John O'Reilly, who makes his career in the military, for sending me the following story.

A few years ago, a group of salesmen went to a regional sales convention in Chicago. They had assured their wives that they would be home in plenty of time for Friday night's dinner. In their rush through the airport, with plane tickets and briefcases in hand, one of the salesmen inadvertently kicked over a table that held a display of fresh apples. Apples flew in every direction. Without stopping or even looking back at the damage, they managed to reach the gate area just in time for boarding their flight. All but one of the men, that is. He paused at the sight of the scattered apples, took a deep breath, got in touch with his feelings, and experienced a twinge of compassion for the girl whose apple stand had been overturned. He caught up with his buddies and told them to go on without him. He asked one of his companions to call his wife upon arrival in their hometown and explain that he would be taking a later flight.

Then the man returned to the area in the terminal where the teenaged girl and her overturned apple stand were. He found her in a state of panic. To his surprise, he discovered that she was totally blind. She was on her knees, softly crying, tears running down her cheeks in frustration, and at the same time helplessly groping for her spilled produce as the passing crowd swirled around her.

The salesman righted the overturned table. Then he knelt on the floor beside the girl and helped her to gather up the apples. He put the fruit back on the table, some battered and bruised by the fall; these he set aside. When they had finished fixing her display he asked the girl, "Are you okay?" She nodded yes through her tears. Then he took out his wallet and said, "Please take this $40 for the damage we did. I hope we didn't spoil your day too much."

As the man began to walk away, the bewildered girl called out to him, "Mister!" He paused and turned to look towards her once more. She asked, "Are you Jesus?"

The second reflection was written by a famous example of the virtue of compassion: Blessed Mother Teresa of Calcutta. It is called "Send Me Someone to Love."

Lord, when I am hungry,
give me someone who stretches out their hand to me;
When I am thirsty,
give me someone who needs a drink;
When I am cold,
give me someone who is numb with cold;
When I am troubled,
give me someone to console.
When my cross becomes heavy,
give me someone to help;
When I feel abandoned,
give me someone to love.[68]

5

Blessed are those who seek justice
for the earth;
their descendants shall flourish

The world is charged with the grandeur of God.
—*Gerard Manley Hopkins*

Whether you agree with the effectiveness of the Kyoto Protocol or not, believe global warming is mainly a natural phenomenon and not the result of humanity's insensitivity to nature, or figure the problems with the environment will go away if you stop thinking about them, there is no getting around the fact that nature, as we know it, is changing – both radically and rapidly. In 2004, *The Globe and Mail* newspaper reported that since 1990, the world has logged the warmest ten years on record. "By the middle of this century, rising temperatures are predicted to trigger an irreversible melting of the Greenland ice cap, the flooding of lowlands worldwide, and the occurrences of other environmental catastrophes that will affect all forms of life on the planet."[69] Scientists agree that if the current rate of global warming and habitat destruction were to continue, half of the species of plants and animals will be gone by the end of the 21st century, leaving our descendants a biologically impoverished world. The Millennium Ecosystem Assessment, conducted in 2005 by 1,300 experts from 95 countries under the auspices of the United Nations, confirmed that the ecological destruction of the last 50 years is greater than all of the damage caused by human beings since our existence on Earth began.

Some suggest that the way business is pursued today – its narrow world view, its isolationism – contributes greatly to our present situation. Business often operates on an uncontested ideology of continuous growth, consumption, competition, and profit for its own sake, and is totally dependent on the burning of fossil fuel.[70]

Even more basic, it seems to me, is the *"domination"* theory of our relationship to nature. Biblically, this theory, or theology, is based on Genesis 1:27-29. After God created humans in the divine image, God blessed them saying: "Be fertile and multiply; and fill the earth and subdue it; and have dominion over the fish of the sea and the birds of the air and over every living thing that moves upon the earth."

The key words here are, of course, "subdue" and "dominion." Behind this theological interpretation is a dichotomy between matter and spirit and the belief that nature has no inherent rights or value. It is also a homocentric perspective towards creation. Writer Satish Kumar describes this position in its modern form:

> The Industrial Revolution, scientific discoveries, and technological inventions have created the illusion that we, the human race, are the rulers, that we can take nature's laws into our own hands, and do what we like with them. We are the masters of creation; we are in charge of the natural world – its forests, rivers, mountains, fishes, fossils, animals, birds, oil, gas, coal.[71]

We think there are no limits to our power because we have invented the computer, split the atom, sent people to the moon. What is missing in this approach to creation is the virtue of humility.

There are two other theologies of creation: *stewardship* and *interrelationship*.

The theology of stewardship stresses our obligation to be thoughtful caretakers of the earth, using natural resources wisely, for they are entrusted to us by the Creator. This is a biocentric perspective towards nature according to environmentalist Thomas Berry. This theology is based on Genesis 2:15, "Then the Lord God took the man and put him in the garden of Eden, to till it and keep it."

Here, the two key words are "till" and "keep." In this view, technologies are evaluated in light of their environmental impact. Sustainability and sustainable development are key aspects of the stewardship approach. Sustainable development is the achievement of continued economic and social development without detriment to the environment and natural resources. The quality of future human activity is increasingly seen as being dependent on maintaining this balance.[72] Sustainability is viewed as a long-term evolutionary commitment. Companies are encouraged to aim continuously to reduce their consumption of natural resources and to develop new products, services, and processes that will help their organization and others to achieve sustainable goals.

Sustainable actions would include water conservation, reducing greenhouse gas emissions, developing alternative fuel sources, increasing solar power and wind energy resources, sponsoring tree planting initiatives, and so on. Stewardship also involves some form of accountability or reporting to make sure the goals sought are being achieved.[73]

The theology of interrelationship rejects notions of domination and moves beyond the approach of stewardship. In this theology, creation has value because of its relationship to God rather than its usefulness for humanity. It is a theocentric perspective towards creation. The biblical basis is also found in the Book of Genesis: "God saw everything that he had made, and indeed, it was very good" (Genesis 1:31; see also Genesis 9, Psalms 104 and 148, and the Book of Job, chapters 38 and 39).

The key word here is "everything." The whole universe was created by God, who delights in what has been created. All creation belongs to a single community; everything is related. In the story of Noah from the Hebrew Scriptures (Old Testament), we see that the covenant the Creator established included more than human beings (see Genesis 9:9-16). Of special note is this sentence: "God said to Noah and his [children], 'I am establishing my covenant with you and your descendants after you, and with every creature that is with you...'" (9:9, 10).

Someone who profoundly grasped the significance of the interrelationship between God and all created beings was Francis of Assisi (1182–1226). Francis experienced a kinship to creatures and a loving relationship with the elements of nature – both animate and inanimate. We see this especially in his "Canticle of Brother Sun." Here is an excerpt:

> All praise be yours, my Lord, through all that you have made,
> And first my lord Brother Sun,
> Who brings the day; and light you give to us through him ...
> All praise be yours, my Lord, through Sister Moon and Stars;
> In the heavens you have made them bright
> And precious and fair ...
> All praise be yours, my Lord, through Sister Water,
> So useful, lowly, precious and pure ...
> All praise be yours, my Lord, through Sister Earth, our mother,
> Who feeds us in her sovereignty and produces
> Various fruits with colored flowers and herbs ...
> Praise and bless my Lord, and give him thanks,
> And serve him with great humility.[74]

St. Francis teaches us that we need to have a reverential attitude toward all of creation. In 1979, Pope John Paul II proclaimed Francis heavenly patron of ecology. In his 1990 Peace Day message, the Pope wrote, "Francis ... offers Christians an example of genuine and deep respect for the integrity of creation."[75] Francis understood the interdependence of creation: that human beings should not see themselves as dominant over nature but as beings who are part of it. This, of course, requires of humans a responsibility to protect the integrity of creation for its own sake, as well as for the welfare of future generations.

One manner of thinking that stands in the way of the theology of interrelationship proclaims a dichotomy between matter and spirit. According to this view, much of nature does not have rights because it is made up of dull matter. Jesuit paleontologist Teilhard de Chardin (1881–1955) addressed this issue in his book *The Future of Man*. He called his theory "the law of complexity-consciousness."

> Everyone has known from the beginning that organized matter is endowed with spontaneity in combination with psychic inwardness. Everyone also knows today that this organic matter is amazingly complicated .... Absolutely inert and totally brute matter *does not exist*. Every element of the universe contains, at least to an infinitesimal degree, some germ of inwardness and spontaneity, that is to say of consciousness.[76]

This "inwardness" is known as the *within* of things. Writer Sean McDonagh explains Teilhard's insight.

> From the first moment of the universe twenty billion years ago, every particle of matter carried within itself the seeds of everything that was to emerge in later unfoldings, including human consciousness ....
>
> According to Teilhard, the galaxies, the solar system, and the earth unfolded through a dramatic variety of sequences – from the initial energy in the "primeval atom," through the synthesization of matter in the first generation of the stars, to the birth of life on planet earth, and finally to human consciousness itself. With the increased complexification of matter through successive transformations, there is a corresponding increase in interiorization.[77]

Teilhard was a prophet as well as a scientist. He was doing his research and writing long before it became popular to show the intimate connection between religion and science. Like any true prophet, he faced opposition to his ideas, especially in the Catholic Church. But his integrity in himself and in his work held fast. His work has influenced many. According to Mircea Eliade, who was a great comparative religion scholar in Teilhard's time, Teilhard was the first Christian author to present his faith in terms accessible and meaningful to the agnostic scientist and to the religiously illiterate in general.

Teilhard's insight contradicts the perspective of those who look at matter and spirit in a dualistic way. By stressing the fundamental unity of life in its inwardness, he gives us a cosmic sensibility to the interrelatedness of all creation. Here, in poetic form, in his "Hymn to Matter," he proclaims his discovery.

> I bless you matter and you I acclaim; not as the pontiffs of science or the moralizing preachers depict you, debased, disfigured – a mass of brute forces and base appetites – but as you reveal yourself to me today, in your totality and your true nature.
>
> You I acclaim as the inexhaustible potentiality for existence and transformation wherein the predestined substance germinates and grows ....
>
> I acclaim you as the divine milieu, charged with creative power, as the ocean stirred by the Spirit, as the clay molded and infused with life by the Incarnate Word.[78]

We can safely say, I believe, that to save our planet we need not only an intellectual transformation through scientific information, but a spiritual awakening as well. We need to leave behind our dominating attitude towards nature, go beyond the stewardship model, and enter fully into understanding ourselves as part of nature, in relationship with it. Connectedness is the basis for an eco-spirituality to counteract eco-destruction. As theologian Elizabeth Johnson suggests, to change the way we treat nature and its gifts we must change our entire cosmology – seeing all of creation as worthy in itself rather than simply serving human beings. In terms of spirituality, this disposition involves an extension of the principle of the common good to include all of creation.

In this communal context, redemption has to do with more than the individual human person. Humanity and the natural world are being saved together. As St. Paul writes, "All of creation waits with eager longing for God to reveal his sons (and daughters) ... there is the hope that creation itself will one day be set free from its slavery to decay and share the glorious freedom of the children of God" (Romans 8:19-21, Good News Bible [GNB]).

Our Response

As we consider what efforts to make on behalf of the environment, we do well to keep in mind Pope John Paul II's comment about St. Francis of Assisi's deep respect for the *integrity of creation*. This is the basic norm of our commitment. The *"Rerum Novarum* Conference," held in 1990 to commemorate the 100th anniversary of the first Roman Catholic social encyclical, presented five principles from which our actions must emerge:

1. Focus on human dignity must be expanded to include the dignity of all creation.
2. The option for the poor must include an "oppressed" earth.
3. The common good is the good of all creation.
4. The image of God is mirrored in the entire universe.
5. Global solidarity must be understood as solidarity with *all* God's creatures.

Jesuit Al Fritsch, who has been an environmental activist for many years, suggests seven viable models for acting justly towards creation.[79] I have amplified each with examples. Some people fit better into one model's framework than another, because of personality, temperament, or even time constraints, and many of us may take on more than one perspective at a given time. Fritsch originally suggested these models for the 1990s; I believe they are just as relevant for the 21st century.

The Caretaker Model or Stewardship Model

Involves watchfulness, care, concern about creation, and stresses personal and corporate responsibility and accountability. This model encompasses such activities as recycling, driving a fuel-efficient vehicle, conserving water, and so forth. In Calgary, I was constantly amazed at the industriousness of the street people who daily walk alleys in the downtown area, collecting cans and bottles to redeem at the Bottle Depot; these men and women are among the most effective recyclers in the city.

More and more businesses are incorporating care for the earth into their code of ethics. Consider, for example, Petro-Canada, a large Canadian oil company. In its code of business conduct, environmental protection is highlighted in this way:

> We are committed to the protection of the environment. We conduct our activities lawfully in a manner that is consistent with sound environmental management and conservation practices and actively pursue ways to minimize the environmental impact of our operations and products.[80]

The challenge, of course, is to abide by these environmental principles on a consistent basis.

A second example of the Caretaker Model is the Green Hotel Association, a worldwide group of hoteliers committed to saving water and energy while reducing waste. Small changes, such as handing out cards to guests to consider using their towels and bedsheets for more than one day, have added to waste reduction. The April 2006 issue of *Calgary Inc.* magazine contains a thirteen-point suggestion on how to create an eco-friendly office. Here are some of the recommendations of this stewardship model.

- Ask your employees to turn off their computers and monitors in the evening; it doesn't harm the computer and it saves energy.
- Set up a recycling program for everything from paper and glass to cardboard, wood and computers.
- When purchasing supplies or equipment, look at the labels (e.g., Ecologo, Energy Star, Forest Stewardship Council) to make sure you're buying environmentally friendly goods.
- Participate in the One-Tonne Challenge program and see how your company can help your employees reduce their individual greenhouse gas emissions by a tonne in a year (e.g., transit incentives, discounted home energy audits).
- Packaging is notorious for generating waste. See if you can do away with it, reuse it, or at least recycle it.
- Consider making your fleet greener with hybrid, biodiesel or electric vehicles.
- Figure out what your biggest environmental impact is and set a target to improve your performance in that area. Communicate your action plan and challenge and reward your employees for their achievements.
- Do the things you do at home at work – turn off lights, turn down the heat, run a full dishwasher, be frugal.[81]

The Partner or Creation-Centred Model

Believes that we have a relationship with Mother Earth; we learn from the earth; we must work in harmony with nature. This model appears in Aboriginal spirituality. Like St. Francis of Assisi, for whom every creature in the world was a mirror of God's presence and, when approached with reverence, was a step leading us to God, many Aboriginal people experience the

Creator revealing himself to them through birds, animals and other aspects of creation. They seek to connect with the divine – called the Great Spirit by some and the Great Mystery by others – through images from nature. Some indigenous people, such as the Guyami Indians of Panama, incorporate intimate connection with the earth with ways of honouring it in their personal lives, in their hymns. Consider their "dawn song."

> From the great rock I see it, the Daybreak Star, the
> sign of the dawning.
> Above the mountain it rises and my heart dances.
> Now the light comes, the light that makes me one
> with all life.
> Like the tinamou I am, who sings in the dawn, who
> is humble with love,
> Let me be like a ray of light, like a flower blazing
> with light,
> Like the waterfall laughing with light, like the great
> tree also,
> Mighty in its roots that split the rocks, mighty in its
> head that reaches the sky,
> And its leaves catch the light and sing with the wind
> a song of the circle.
> Let my life be like the rainbow, whose colors teach
> us unity;
> Let me follow always the great circle, the roundness
> of power,
> … all the circles of life, and whose command is like
> the thunder:
> "Be kind, be kind, be brave, be brave, be pure, be pure,
> Be humble as the earth, and be as radiant as the
> sunlight!"
> Amen.[82]

We live out the Creation-Centred model with such activities as Earth Day, conservation projects, and species protection programs, each of which helps lower the impact of human beings on nature, limiting our environmental footprint on Mother Earth.

The Suffering Servant Model

Sees the earth as wounded, in need of humble service, and understands the intimate connection between social poverty and ecological poverty, that the "cry of the Earth" is also the "cry of the people." Writer Jane Blewett describes the situation well in her article "Impoverished People, Impoverished Earth":

> ... it is they [the poor and minorities] who are paying the higher price for our planet in peril. It is in their communities that landfills are being located, toxic wastes dumped, incinerators built, highways cutting through to create mega thruways that won't serve their needs. It is the children of the poor who are being brain-damaged from eating lead paint and poisoned foods .... It is their homes that bear disproportionately high energy costs because they are not insulated or wired well. And it is not only poor people in the United States [and Canada], but whole nations [in the developing world] who now must destroy their resource base, their forests and soil, to repay debts to the rich First World ....[83]

Speaking in religious terms, we are talking here about sin. Not just personal sin, which accounts for individual moral transgressions, or social sin – structural injustices of organizations and nations that violate the dignity of people and their aspirations – but cosmic sin. Cosmic sins are offences against nature. Such assaults on creation as deforestation, the use of harmful pesticides, air and water pollution, the irresponsibility of driving gas-guzzling vehicles, strip mining, and toxic waste are threats to the very integrity of creation. The other side of sin is, of course, salvation. Here I draw on an enlightening article by Elaine Siemsen entitled "Who is the Cosmic Christ?"

In the first few centuries after Jesus' resurrection, the community of believers described the meaning of the Easter events in many ways. These efforts are called Christology, which is the term used to describe the study of the person and work of Christ. In the early church, Christ was seen as the ransom for sin, the sacrificial lamb and the model of the life in God. Each Christology celebrated the gift of God in Jesus Christ for our salvation. In their diversity, all agreed that the foundation of salvation was in the origins of creation. God made humanity and the cosmos, and God saves humanity and all of the cosmos.

Joseph Sittler, a noted Lutheran theologian, wrote in 1952 that the Christian community needed to carefully examine the limitations placed upon the work of the Christ: "It is now excruciatingly clear that Christ cannot be a light that lighteth everyone coming into the world, if he is not also the light that falls upon the world into which everyone comes."[84]

God's work of redemption in Jesus encompasses all that is created. In the Gospel of Mark, Jesus tells his disciples, "Go into all the world and proclaim the good news to the whole creation" (16:15). The Suffering Servant Model, then, recognizes sin and salvation, failure and grace, woundedness and redemption.

The Good Samaritan Model

Sees the wounded condition of plants and animals and all of God's creatures, and takes an active and advocating role in initiating the healing process; is aware of the interconnectedness of all beings.

We saw in Chapter 4 that one of the key virtues in Jesus' story of the Good Samaritan (Luke 10:25-37) is compassion. The Samaritan takes time from his busy schedule to tend to the wounds of a man who lies in the dirt, beaten by thieves, and left to die. In the Good Samaritan Model, we are asked to tend to the woundedness of our planet not as something separate from ourselves, but as part of who we are. Albert Einstein had something to say about this point:

> Human beings are a part of a whole called by us "the universe," a part limited in time and space. We experience ourselves, our thoughts and feelings, as something separated from the rest – a kind of optical delusion of consciousness. The delusion is a kind of prison for us, restricting us to our personal desire and to affection for a few persons nearest to us. Our task must be to free ourselves from this prison by widening our circles of compassion to embrace all living creatures and the whole of nature in its beauty.[85]

We have entered a new age, suggests Thomas Berry and other environmentalists: the *Ecozoic Age*. In his book *The Great Work: Our Way into the Future*, Berry writes about previous ages.[86] For example, the Classical Period introduced ideas of reason, democracy, and philosophy into human consciousness. The medieval period saw the building of great cathedrals. The Age of Discovery opened lines of travel and communication around the world. The Technological Age revolutionized our way of communicating and acquiring knowledge. However, our technological power has also had its impact on the environment, often leaving a nasty environmental footprint.

In the Ecozoic Age, we must re-establish the connection our ancient ancestors had to nature, and work towards sustainable lifestyles that reverse the destruction human beings are currently inflicting on the planet. As Berry writes, "We must learn that we are a communion of subjects, not a collection of objects."[87]

In his book, Berry details where efforts are being made to give credit to people whose vision exemplifies the Ecozoic. One person who embodies this vision is John McCarthy. John is a Jesuit priest who has a Ph.D. in Forest Ecology. As he tells it, he fell in love with the forest at an early age, gripped by the natural wonders of Newfoundland, where he grew up. His favourite forest is a stand of old-growth boreal wood on the Great Northern Peninsula of Newfoundland. It includes the watershed of the beautiful Main River, the province's first entry in the system of Canadian Heritage Rivers. (Newfoundland's Bay du Nord River was nominated in 2006 for Heritage River Status; that makes two heritage rivers for the province.) There is more to this river than its beauty, though. Its watershed is part of one of the last remnants of boreal old-growth forest in the Province. Reflecting on his experience, John says, "I feel that my research has opened up a new vision of the forest, not only in scientific terms, but also in terms of how we view forests from an affective, moral, and spiritual perspective."[88] Being a realist as well as a man deeply committed to the sanctity of the environment, John recognizes the constant demand of the province for wood fibre.

Logging companies and the pulpwood industry think in terms of "harvesting" the old-growth forest. However, a "harvest" suggests that a forest is a crop no different from those grown on farms. John is concerned with what he sees as a uni-dimensional view of the forest. In addition to the use of wood fibre for commercial reasons, other values, such as biological diversity and the cultural significance of forests and the wilderness, need to be taken into consideration. While he does not completely oppose tree cutting, he believes that a balance with biological integrity and sustainability must be kept. As he argues, "I can sympathize with the loggers, but I know that if given access to these last remaining virgin old-growth forests, they will very soon run out of wood again and we will have lost a significant patrimony."[89]

John's commitment to save the forests is a personal matter, both academically and spiritually. He sums up his vision:

We gaze out on creation and witness the loss and death we have unleashed.

We witness the loss of beauty, of countless images and experiences provided by the diversity of forests and wild places. As the trees fall and the hills are laid bare, our human hearts, both individual and collective, are pierced. I wonder if the source of our lament is rooted in the acknowledgement, be it explicit or unconscious, that our current rapacious relationship with the world's forests is inherently dehumanizing and contrary to the human spirit.[90]

The Teacher Model

Consists of environmental education professionals who develop educational materials or administer or teach in formal settings. They endeavour to describe or explain the current political, social, or economic situation, and to raise the consciousness of their students and the general public.

An abundance of educational resources is available, from foundations such as David Suzuki's to government and non-governmental support groups. I Googled "environmental educators" and up came myriad organizations. These include magazines such as *Corporate Knights*, a Canadian publication for ethically responsible businesses, and *Spiritearth*, a US monthly whose focus is "contemplation, reflection and justice-making for the ecozoic era." Most mainstream magazines, such as *Time*, *Newsweek*, and *Fortune*, have published special features on care for the environment.

Time emphasized global warming in its April 3, 2006, issue. *Calgary Inc.*'s April 2006 issue featured the article "Will Calgary Ever Be Green?", which serves to raise the consciousness of one city to a greater understanding of the challenges that lie before it, and gives practical suggestions on how to improve its responsibility to the environment.

More and more conferences are being held throughout the world on eco-spirituality, eco-system health, global warming, and sustainability concerns. The number of quality books on the environment, relating to both its blessings and the challenges facing it, are on the increase. We have come a long way since Teilhard de Chardin did his research and writing, but we have a long way to go to move our collective will to long-term effective action. One reason for our hesitance is the need for sacrifice: individual and corporate, local and national, and global. Some of us are more reluctant than others to go that route. Nature retreats – educational resources that touch the soul as well as the mind – can help people find the will to take action.

I have given retreats in nature since the mid 1980s, and have found them a profound way of connecting to creation. By reflecting on the beauty of nature in the context of the Creator's bountiful love, as well as reflecting on some of the attacks against the environment by human beings (including ourselves), we can come to a deeper awareness that we are part of an interrelationship with nature. I am indebted to Colm Lavelle, an Irish Jesuit priest who has been conducting nature retreats in Ireland for many years, for some of the prayer exercises I use on these retreats. My inspiration comes from Jesus Christ, who used many examples from nature in his parables about the kingdom of God: salt of the earth, sheep and wolves, seed for sowing, sheep and goats, lilies of the field, weeds among wheat, a barren fig tree, a net full of fish, a mustard seed, a vineyard.

I am also indebted to Francis of Assisi and to his most faithful disciple, Claire of Assisi, for whom every creature was a mirror of God's presence, and, if approached with reverence, a step leading us to God.[91] The following contemplative prayer exercise is one I use on nature retreats.

*

A Nature Prayer Exercise

- Take a leisurely, quiet stroll out in the country or in a park, near the ocean or by a lake, in a mountain area or a desert, or perhaps in your own backyard. Try not to analyze what you are seeing, hearing, smelling, feeling. Just be at peace in God's creation.
- If you feel inclined to sit or lie down, do so.
- If you feel moved to sing or hum, or make up your own psalm of praise for the beauty around you, fine.

- As you walk, or sit, or lie down, be aware of the sights and sounds, even of the silence around you and in you.
- Now let some object in nature choose you – anything you can hold in your hand that exists in its natural state: a rock, a leaf, a twig, a flower, a weed, a pine needle, an acorn, a feather, a shell, etc.
- Reverently begin to explore this piece of creation with your fingers. Feel its texture. Be aware of how heavy or light it is. Pass it across your ear and listen to its sound. Draw it close to your nose and inhale its scent. Touch it to your lips and, if safe, taste it with the tip of your tongue.
- Next, moving a bit into the analytical, you may wish to be the object in your imagination.
- Listen to it: Is it saying something to you about yourself? About life? About the Creator? About its existence? What are you saying to God as the object? What is God saying to you through it?
- Finally, express your gratitude to God in some way for this time of prayer in nature.

*

I have used this prayer exercise with a variety of groups, from men and women at a picturesque retreat centre in San Diego, California, to a group of men in inner-city Belfast, Northern Ireland. It never ceases to amaze me how profound an experience this is as people let go of a need to control an event with the rational mind, and allow their intuition to emerge.

If it is a stormy day outside, or if illness prohibits your going out, choose a room in your home where you can be quiet and free of distractions. Reflectively consider something in the room that is made from natural materials, such as wood, and apply whatever is appropriate in the above prayer exercise. For example, a chair or a window frame may be made of wood. If you have an indoor plant, you could make it the instrument of your prayer. Or you can look outside a window and contemplate the beauty of nature. One businessman told me that the view from his office takes in the Canadian Rockies at a distance. He shared how, periodically, he pauses to gaze at the view, which gives him a sense of inner peace in the midst of an otherwise hectic day.

The purpose of the nature prayer exercise is threefold: to draw you closer to the Creator, to make you more appreciative of the Creator's handiwork, and to help you learn something more about yourself. It can be a rich learning experience: the teacher is nature.

The Activist Model

Realizes that threats to the environment need social analysis in order to determine the underlying economic, political, and social forces that lead to eco-destruction; is willing to take a pro-active, rather than passive, stance towards the serious problems facing the world; and is willing to challenge the status quo of a company, a city, a nation; is especially concerned with the injustices perpetrated against nature, and works for justice in co-operation with other like-minded people.

There are many environmental activist groups in existence, and more emerging as this book goes to print. Some are concerned with energy conservation and minimizing one's ecological footprint. Others want to protect, restore, and enhance the natural capital of trees and forests. Still others are concerned with protecting all native wild animals and plants, with special emphasis on the threat of species extinction and the loss of biological diversity. Some activities are aimed at the local scene; others are directed to the global arena.

The Center of Concern, a Catholic lobby organization based in Washington, DC, integrates social analysis with theological reflection in its efforts for a more just and environmentally sound world. Since 1971, it has been enabling individuals, organizations, and coalitions to explore and analyze global issues and social structures from an ethical perspective based on Catholic social teaching. In addition to its emphasis on connecting analysis with spirituality and theology, the Center operates on several fronts to bring its vision to reality. It articulates a call to justice for the faith community; critiques policy for those in leadership and for the general public; links environmental issues to those who suffer the most from eco-destruction – the economically poor – giving the voiceless a voice at the tables of power; provides leadership and moral vision to advocacy networks working for more just institutions and policies in the United States and in the international arena; supports grassroots justice movements; and provides education on critical domestic and international issues.

Sometimes an activist emerges from an unexpected quarter. At the time of the following occurrence, Judy Martz was governor of Montana. The difficulty she encountered started with a badly planned strategy by the premier of British Columbia, who wanted to exploit coal-bed methane – natural gas trapped in coal seams – in southern BC in order to help offset a $38-billion provincial debt.[92] However, to coax methane out of coal requires a frightening amount of surface land disturbance, more than that needed for conventional gas, as well as the dewatering of underground coalfields. Disposing of this water, which is often contaminated, can be messy. Yet BC Premier Gordon Campbell decided to go ahead with the project anyway. So he put two big blocks of coal-rich wilderness along the Flathead River up for sale.

Governor Martz heard about this get-rich-quick scheme. Concerned that coal-bed methane developments might dump polluted waters into the headwaters of the Flathead River, and thereby despoil popular US Glacier National Park, she asked that BC postpone the auction until a proper baseline environmental study could be conducted. Montana's 2003 final impact statement on coal-bed methane lays out a long list of problems, including degraded surface waters, polluted air, and the loss of 70,000 acres of grazing land. When her appeals fell on deaf BC ears, she wrote to Ottawa requesting a federal environmental assessment. She also referred to the 1909 Boundary Waters Treaty, which clearly states that boundary waters "shall not be polluted on either side to the injury of health or property on the other."

By now, BC's behaviour had alarmed even the coal-bed methane industry. In the end, a Montana–BC alliance, representing communities on both sides of the border who were sympathetic to Governor Martz's concerns, took their case to Calgary energy giants EnCana, Devon, and Shell Canada. The alliance politely asked the firms not to bid on the leases at the auction and to press for proper studies. The companies got the message. They tallied up the environmental risks plus the social costs, and, in the end, no one put in a bid. Local communities and industry showed they could work together for the betterment of the environment. This positive outcome came from the persistent courage of Judy Martz.

The Prophetic Model

Sees the cosmic sin that threatens the integrity of creation and speaks publicly, verbally, by the written word, or through the media to expose the root causes of environmental destruction, demanding social change. The prophet is willing to act alone, accepts nonconformity as part of the price, and does not expect to be liked, respected, or applauded. Prophets must beware of becoming isolated from their base community of co-believers, whom they need for stability and strength.

Prophecy plays a major role in the Hebrew Scriptures. Prophets such as Isaiah, Jeremiah, Hosea, and Micah appeared at critical moments in the nation of Israel's history, calling the people back to God and God's way after they had strayed. The English word "prophet" is derived from the Greek *prophetes*, which means "one who speaks before others."

Prophets are countercultural and, therefore, often controversial. Their message may make us uncomfortable. They are not intimidated by charges of political incorrectness.

Modern environmental pioneer prophets have many faces. I want to mention three in particular: John Muir, Henry Thoreau, and Rachel Carson. On their shoulders, more recent outspoken men and women rest.

John Muir (1838–1914), a tenacious Scot, was a naturalist, a writer, and the founder of the Sierra Club. He has been called "The Father of our National Parks" and "Wilderness Prophet." He was a wilderness explorer in California's Sierra Nevada, among Alaska's glaciers, and abroad. His writings are an important part of America's heritage because of his deep spiritual insight into the integrity of creation, and his efforts to communicate the importance of protecting America's natural surroundings. He continues to be an inspiration for those concerned with threats to the environment.

Henry Thoreau (1817–1862), like Muir, lived for long spells amidst nature. According to Randall Conrad, director of the Thoreau Project, Thoreau dedicated his life to the exploration of nature not as a backdrop to human activity, but as a living, integrated system of which human beings are simply one part. Conrad also comments on Thoreau's professional development – his "nature writing" progressed from the poetic symbolism of his classic book *Walden* to the scientific method used in his later journals. Thoreau was a man of great principles and tremendous courage.

Both Muir and Thoreau, Thomas Berry points out, believed that the human species was part of the larger community of life – not the centre of it – and that a mutually enhancing bond between humanity and nature is necessary for the true enrichment of human beings.[93] Each also recognized the intimate connection between nature's welfare and our own. Berry notes that, in their time, only such wilderness adventurers as Muir and Thoreau were aware that the diminishment of the grandeur and fertility of the natural world weakened the entire biosphere, eliminated a profound psychic experience, restricted imaginative power for human beings, and bereaved them of unique experiences of divine presence.[94]

Born when Muir was 69 years old, Rachel Carson (1907–1964) was a biologist, writer, and ecologist. She grew up in a simple farmhouse outside the western Pennsylvania river town of Springdale. She credited her mother with introducing her to the world of nature. After completing her education, she joined the US Bureau of Fisheries as a writer of a radio show entitled "Romance Under the Waters," in which she was able to explore life under the seas and bring it to listeners. She wrote books on her observations of life under the sea and pamphlets on conservation and natural resources.

In 1954 she wrote, "The more we can focus our attention on the wonders and realities of the universe about us, the less taste we shall have for destruction."

Her focus changed reluctantly, according to biographer Linda Lear; when disturbed by the profligate use of synthetic chemical pesticides after World War II, she began warning the public about the long-term effects of misusing pesticides.[95] In her book groundbreaking 1962 book, *Silent Spring*, Carson challenged the practices of agricultural scientists and the government, and called for a change in the way humankind viewed the natural world. Her perspective challenged the theology of domination. Like the prophets of old, she experienced persecution for her beliefs. Linda Lear relates that the chemical industry and some in government dismissed Carson as an alarmist, but she courageously spoke out to remind them (and us) that we are a vulnerable part of the natural world, subject to the same damage as the rest of the ecosystem. Testifying before Congress in 1963, she called for new policies to protect human health and the environment. Embedded within all her writings (and testimony) was the view that human beings are but one part of nature and that we live in relationship with all of creation.

Like Carson, many prophets were reluctant to speak out on issues, to take on the establishment, but as in the case of Jeremiah in the Hebrew scriptures, a "fire" burns within and the prophet is compelled to raise the awareness of others. In Carson's case, her belief in the integrity of creation and her compassion for humanity set the fire going in her.

Three women who would be considered more recent prophets are Dorothy Day, Helen Caldicott, and Jackie Flanagan. Prophets are visionaries; their utterances often make the rest of us uncomfortable. It is said of Dorothy Day, for example, that her mission was to "comfort the afflicted and afflict the comfortable." As Jesus learned in Nazareth, prophets have a hard time being accepted in their own town, city, or country.

Dorothy Day, who died in 1980, was a tireless defender of the poor and the downtrodden, and a true champion of peace. Grounded in the Sermon on the Mount, she was a woman of prayer and action. She fasted, protested, suffered humiliation, and spent time in prison for her beliefs. She once said, "The greatest challenge of the day is how to bring about a revolution of the heart, a revolution which has to start with each one of us."[96] I am convinced that were she alive today, she would be pointing out to us the intimate connection between threats to the environment and the plight of those who are the most severely affected by eco-destruction: the poor.

Helen Caldicott, an Australian physician, has devoted most of her life to an international campaign regarding some of the primary hazards of the nuclear age. Not only is she an expert in her field, but, like Dorothy Day, she puts her ideas into action. She is co-founder of Physicians for Social Responsibility, an organization of over 23,000 doctors, and the founder of International Physicians to Save the Environment. Caldicott was born in Melbourne, Australia, where she received her medical degree in 1961 from the University of Adelaide Medical School. In 1977, she joined the staff of the Children's Hospital Medical Center in Boston and taught pediatrics at the Harvard Medical

School. She left her medical career in 1980, setting her sights on calling the world's attention to the madness of nations making and stockpiling nuclear weapons. She campaigned against Hershey Foods Corporation: its Philadelphia factory used milk from local dairy cows, producing chocolate containing strontium 90 following the nearby Three Mile Island nuclear accident in 1979. Caldicott is a woman of great conviction, not afraid to challenge the policies of a business, an industry, or a government. Two of her most recent books are *The New Nuclear Danger: George W. Bush's Military Industrial Complex* (2001) and *Metal of Dishonor: How Depleted Uranium Penetrates Steel, Radiates People and Contaminates the Environment* (1997).

Jackie Flanagan, born and raised in the province of Alberta, Canada, has the fierce determination for justice of her Irish ancestors. In 1998, she started *Alberta Views*, a monthly magazine that deals with the political, social, and cultural debate in western Canada. She says one of the main reasons behind founding this publication was her concern about what the Alberta government had been doing to the province's infrastructure. The conservative perspective of the elected officials, which favours developing the province's bountiful natural resources with a nod now and then to the environment, deeply disturbed her. Jackie is not afraid to take on the establishment, be it government, business, or the churches. *Alberta Views* has covered such issues as the scarcity of water and the need to conserve it; the social and environmental upheaval resulting from the oil "gold rush" in the oil sands in and around Fort McMurray, in the north of the Province; the poor treatment of people with mental illness in the province; the overrepresentation of Aboriginal people in the province's prisons; barriers to women in the workplace; the politics of food; and the crisis facing health care. Her interests are varied, but they all have one thing in common – the need for critical appraisal. She is truly countercultural, in the best sense of that term, while at the same time fully committed to advancing culture in all its forms. Maude Barlow of the Council of Canadians writes, "*Alberta Views* is doing something unique at a time when many media have bowed to corporate influence, addressing its readers as empowered citizens in a democratic society."[97]

Former Vice-President of the United States Al Gore is a prophet in his own right, courageously adding much to our understanding of the perils facing the planet through his award-winning film *An Inconvenient Truth*.

Poetry Fuels Motion

Given the seriousness of environmental issues, the world clearly needs a range of approaches to tackle the questions raised: from an eco-spirituality linked to an eco-theology to complement and augment social analysis, to a commitment to effective action for justice. We also need the intuitive instincts of artists and poets to inspire us. We experienced the giftedness of such people earlier in this chapter – through the mystical lenses of Francis of Assisi's "Canticle of Brother Sun," Teilhard de Chardin's "Hymn to Matter," and the Guyami "Dawn Song." In the Nature Prayer Exercise, we learned that we can compose our own psalm or poem as we walk through the woods, climb a mountain, fish by a river, gaze out at the sea, or simply sit in our own backyard and contemplate God's gift of creation around us. Gerard Manley Hopkins, an English Jesuit and poet (1844–1889), had a distinctive and penetrating way of reflecting on reality. In "God's Grandeur," he laments injuries to nature while at the same time expressing a sense of hope.

> The world is charged with the grandeur of God.
> It will flame out, like shining from shook foil;
> It gathers to a greatness, like the ooze of oil
> Crushed. Why do men then now not reck his rod?
> Generations have trod, have trod, have trod;
> And all is seared with trade, bleared, smeared with toil;
> And wears man's smudge and shares man's smell; the soil
> Is bare now, nor can foot feel, being shod.

And for all this, nature is never spent;
There lives the dearest freshness deep down things;
And though the last light off the Black West went
Oh, morning, at the brown brink eastward, springs –
Because the Holy Ghost over the bent
World broods with warm breast and with ah! bright
wings.[98]

We seek justice for the earth – not only for our own benefit, but for those who will follow us on this planet. The following poem by Edward Matchett shares this perspective:

Let us make a thing of beauty
That long may live when we are gone;
Let us make a thing of beauty
That hungry souls may feast upon;

Whether it be wood or marble
Music, art, or poetry,
Let us make a thing of beauty
To help set man's bound spirit free.[99]

Or, as a Native American proverb says,

We do not inherit the earth from our ancestors,
We borrow it from our children.

6

Blessed are those who are able to forgive; for they will be forgiven

Forgiveness ... always goes beyond what is just and due.
It is not a matter of justice but an affair of grace.
—Richard A. Norris

The greatest lesson I have ever learned about the virtue of forgiveness came to me one Palm Sunday. I was prayerfully reading the Last Supper account in the Gospel of John as preparation for Holy Week. At the time, I was living in a community with twelve other Jesuits. As I reflected on the extraordinary act of Jesus the Master washing his disciples' feet, as a servant would, I was particularly struck by his words to them after he finished:

> "Do you know what I have done to you? You call me Teacher and Lord – and you are right, for that is what I am. So if I, your Lord and Teacher, have washed your feet, you also ought to wash one another's feet. I have set you an example, that you also should do as I have done to you." (John 13:12-15)

What caught my attention was that these words were spoken to men who in a short while would either betray or deny him, or run away and hide for fear of the authorities. This thought got me thinking about forgiveness and about one of the members of my community. Phil and I had had a falling out about three months earlier. What had originally been some kind of minor misunderstanding had become a major barrier between us, because we hadn't sat down and resolved it. As I read this scripture, I asked myself, "What would it mean for me to 'wash' Phil's feet?" The answer came swift and clear: "Go talk to him about this rift in your friendship and be reconciled." At first I hesitated, not knowing what Phil's response might be. So I prayed for the courage to take the initiative. This I was able to do. Phil was a bit wary at the start, but as we discussed the root cause of our dispute, he relaxed. We had an excellent sharing and then found it easy to ask for the other's forgiveness. It was a graced moment as our friendship was restored.

I use this question – "What would it mean for me to wash this person's feet?" – whenever I sense a distance between myself and someone else. The result of my acting on the answer has always been positive.

A variation on this method of forgiving came from a religious sister I once met on a retreat I gave at her congregation's mother house. On each day of the six-day retreat, I gave a presentation on a spiritual topic to about 40 of the sisters. One day I shared some reflections on the beatitude on peacemaking, including the question about washing the feet of someone we are in conflict with. This one sister came to see me afterwards and told me that she and another sister had had a disagreement many years before; they hadn't spoken to each other since. I asked her if the other sister was also on this retreat, and, if so, whether the two of them could find a way to resolve their differences. She explained that the sister was indeed on the property, but not in the way I imagined. She was buried in the community cemetery.

That afternoon, the sister went to the back of the property, found the gravesite of the other sister, and engaged in a forgiving prayer exercise. In her imagination, she apologized to the deceased sister and asked her forgiveness for what she had done to contribute to their falling out. When she came to see me the next day, she described the experience. She felt a great sense of relief, and had the feeling that the other sister had forgiven her, too.

These two examples point to two important aspects of the virtue of forgiveness:

- Forgiveness is a true gift to the other person.
- One of the main persons who benefits in forgiving is the one who forgives.

My action is a gift of peace to the other. I give to the other my time, the emotional energy it took to get to this point, my attention, my concern, and my respect. These, I believe, I gave to Phil, though I only realized so afterwards. The emotional distance that comes from an unforgiven hurt is toxic, and it infects both parties. In an excellent treatment on forgiveness, spiritual writer Lewis Smedes suggests that we forgive another in Four Stages:

The first stage is *hurt* – when someone causes you pain so deep and so unfair that you cannot forget it.

The second stage is *hate* – you cannot shake the memory of how much you hurt and you cannot wish your "enemy" well; you may even hope he or she is suffering as much as you are.

The third stage is *healing* – you are given the insight to see the person who hurt you in a new light. Your memory is healed; you turn back the flow of pain and are free again.

The fourth stage is *the coming together* – you invite the person who hurt you back into your life; if he or she comes honestly, love can move you both toward a new and healed relationship. If the other is unable to come back, you must be healed alone.[100]

Allow me to illustrate each of these stages with a story.

Stage 1: Hurt

Steve is a business consultant and executive coach. In this account he shares an experience of betrayal and the struggle to forgive those responsible.

> Seventeen years ago, I worked for a management consulting firm. The leadership of the company was a husband-and-wife team. During my employment there, I was well regarded by the couple and by my clients. I even invested some of my money in the company. I left the firm after five years, however, because I discovered there was a lack of accountability as to the income the company was generating. So I asked management to buy back my shares. I explained to them why I was leaving, told them about the lack of transparency I had experienced, and moved on.
>
> For the next ten years, I worked in private industry, in human resources. My duties included performance management, organizational development, and employment counselling.
>
> One day, I was approached by the new president of the consulting firm I had worked for ten years previously. According to this person, the company was in danger of losing a contract with their biggest account. Since I had had this same account when I had worked for them, and had a good relationship with the people there (and had kept in touch with some of them over the intervening years), they had come to the conclusion that I was the only person who could help them. I realize now they appealed to a weakness I have: vanity. I am also an absolute sucker for a lost cause. So, I agreed to work for the company again.
>
> After awhile, though, I discovered that the company was withholding some important information from me when they hired me back. The most serious was the damaging behaviour of my predecessor; I had to rebuild the trust lost between the client and the consulting company. I also found

out that the client had specifically asked that I be brought back to handle the account.

During this second time at the consulting firm, I was able to re-establish a good relationship with the client in question, plus bring in another big account.

Thus, I thought all was well with management.

One day, the president called me into her office for a "chat." She told me that revenues had dropped and she was concerned for the solvency of the company.

Actually, our profits were down, but still there.

A month later, we had a board-meeting. There were three people at the meeting besides me. The atmosphere in the room was hostile and disrespectful towards me. It seemed they were blaming me for the drop in revenue, even though the account I had been hired to rescue was doing quite well. It was at that moment that I realized I had been used. I asked the members of the Board to think over the weekend if they felt they could continue to work with me. On the following Monday morning they told me they did not feel they could. I offered my resignation, which they accepted.

Healing from the shabby way I had been treated by the members of the Board came slowly. Feelings of being betrayed stayed with me for quite some time, so deep was the hurt. One day while I was praying about this situation, I relived the fateful Board meeting in my memory. As I did so, I imagined Jesus in the room with us. His presence had a calming effect on my heart and spirit. So powerful was his presence that I found myself able to forgive the three people involved. Now, months later, I harbour no resentment. And I learned a lot from the experience, about myself – about my weaknesses and how to guard myself from falling into them.

In this account we learn about two more important aspects of the virtue of forgiveness:

- Forgiveness does not mean allowing another to take advantage of me.
- Forgiveness does not mean excusing my own or another's conduct.

Stage 2: Hate

This story is from my own life. It may seem unusual to read about a Catholic priest experiencing this emotion, but experience it I did. Here is what happened.

A few years ago I was missioned to a parish that was without a resident pastor. The parish is located in a rural area, and I lived alone in the "priest's house." I had never lived alone for more than a month in my life, nor had I served in a country parish before. There were many other challenges to living there in the first year: new place, new people, and a different climate than I was used to. Thankfully, with God's help and the support of the parishioners, I managed, and gradually adjusted. At the beginning of the second year, the diocesan office sent a Catholic deacon and his wife out to the parish to assist me, because by then I had picked up two additional parishes.

The couple lived in a house close to where I was staying. What was intended to be a helping hand, though, turned out to be a nightmare. The husband was the most difficult person I had ever met. I found him to be belligerent, controlling, lacking in social graces, and intent on taking over the whole parish. Every day was a battle with him, with ever new and unsettling challenges. For example, he had a key to my house, since the offices were in the front of it. In the first couple of months of this arrangement, whenever I would leave for an overnight trip to the nearest city – for a day off and time to buy some provisions – I would come home to find something missing from my office. What he was doing, I discovered, was setting up a separate office in the house where he and his wife lived. When I would confront him about these thefts, a battle of wills would ensue. Being an eternal optimist, I hoped that things would improve over time, but they didn't. What I can acknowledge now is that I grew in emotional strength by standing my ground with this man and not letting his bullying personality overwhelm me. What I didn't expect was how deeply negative I came to feel towards him. One day I realized that I actually hated him. This was a new feeling for me, and was so intense that I could taste it emotionally. During my annual eight-day retreat that year, I shared these feelings with a Jesuit friend of mine, and, with his help, began the long process of healing. It took some months, but eventually I was able to forgive the man. However, I knew I could never trust him.

I learned two important lessons from this experience:

- Forgiveness does not always mean forgetting what happened.
- Reconciliation is not always possible, and that's okay.

Lewis Smedes makes it clear that forgiving doesn't always mean forgetting. If the person you are able to forgive has an abusive personality and is still somehow in your life, your first obligation is to protect yourself from possible further abuse.[101]

Healing the hate results in the forgiver being healed emotionally, which I experienced. I came to the place where I could pray for the well-being of this difficult man while, at the same time, never desire to work with him again.

Stage 3: Healing

In this story, the healing happened on a group level. It took place in the year 1944, in Moscow, as a procession of 20,000 German war prisoners was being marched through the city. Yevgeny Yevtushenko, a beloved Russian poet, witnessed the following incident. Here is his description.

The pavements swarmed with onlookers, cordoned off by soldiers and police. The crowd was mostly women – Russian women with hands roughened by hard work, lips untouched by lipstick and with thin, hunched shoulders which had borne half of the burden of the war.

Every one of them must have had a father or a husband, a brother or a son killed by the Germans.

They gazed with hatred in the direction from which the column was to appear.

At last we saw it.

The generals marched at the head, massive chins stuck out, lips folded disdainfully, their whole demeanour meant to show superiority over their plebeian victors.

"They smell of eau-de-cologne, the bastards," someone in the crowd said with hatred.

The women were clenching their fists. The soldiers and policemen had all they could do to hold them back.

All at once, something happened to them.

They saw German soldiers, thin, unshaven, wearing dirty, bloodstained bandages, hobbling on crutches or leaning on the shoulders of their comrades; the soldiers walked with their heads down.

The street became dead silent – the only sound was the shuffling of boots and the thumping of crutches.

Then I saw an elderly woman in broken-down boots push herself forward and touch a policeman's shoulder, saying, "Let me through." There must have been something about her that made him step aside.

She went up to the column, took from inside her coat something wrapped in a coloured handkerchief and unfolded it.

It was a crust of black bread. She pushed it awkwardly into the pocket of a soldier, so exhausted that he was tottering on his feet. And now suddenly from every side women were running towards the soldiers, pushing into their hands bread, cigarettes, whatever they had.

The soldiers were no longer enemies.

They were people.[102]

Here the lesson is this:

- Forgiveness sometimes requires that the injured person, or persons, take the *first step* for healing to happen. And that takes courage.

Stage 4: Coming together

I take the story for this stage from a very good friend of mine, now in his early 80s, who came from a large family.

My siblings and I were estranged from one another for many years. The problem started when I was made executor of our mother's will. Hard feelings seemed to arise out of nowhere. What once was a close-knit family became splintered and separated. It took a long time and a lot of emotional suffering before we were able to come together again as a family.

One of my nieces broke the ice. She had become increasingly unhappy because of the alienation she experienced from her cousins, and so she approached her father (my brother-in-law) and asked if there couldn't be some closure to the bitterness and separation. He told her he was open to a visit from me. So I went to see him at his home, and we had a tearful reunion. The visit was very positive and spiritually profound for both of us.

Next, the wife of another brother – who heard of this reconciliation – called me and invited me to their house. This brother was very sick – bed-ridden, actually.

He was so ill that he could barely speak. His whole family was there, all hoping and praying for some kind of reconciliation. When I was brought into his bedroom I went straight to him and embraced him. I told him how blessed it was to be a family again. His response, like my brother-in-law's, was very positive. Soon after, this brother was moved to a hospice. Again, I went to see him. When I arrived, his wife asked me to read a passage from the Bible. I wasn't prepared, but I picked up the Bible and found myself looking into the First Letter of John and his reflections on love. This is what I read:

> We love because God first loved us. If someone says he loves God, but hates his brother [or sister], he is a liar. For he cannot love God, whom he has not seen, if he does not love his brother [or sister] whom he has seen. The command that Christ has given us is this: whoever loves God must love his brother [or sister] also. (1 John 4:19-21, GNB)

Now I realize how much God was a part of this whole process of reconciliation, for it is clear to me that the Holy Spirit guided me to this scripture passage.

The lesson for us here is:

• Forgiveness does not mean being immediately free of all anger and resentment. Sometimes it takes many years and many tears to get there.

My friend Father Jim Hanley summarizes the steps to forgiveness in this succinct way:

1. Recognize the pain the other has caused within me.
2. Admit any responsibility on my part.

3. Look at the person who hurt me as God sees that individual.

4. Imagine what God wants for that person and try to desire the same.

5. Let go of the person and turn him or her over to God for healing and growth.

6. Reflect on the forgiveness God has given to me.

7. Realize the negative effects of non-forgiveness in my life.

8. Repeat the above steps daily in prayer.[103]

Forgiveness Explored

People have reflected on the theme of forgiveness since ancient times. The Bible contains countless stories of God's mercy towards human beings. Plenty of passages encourage people to forgive one another. However, what was once mostly spoken from the pulpit is now found in mainstream society.

There are books on healing of memories of past hurts – some that go back to early childhood, but inhibit a person from acting holistically in the present; how-to books that give steps necessary for forgiveness to take root; treatises on forgiving oneself; and institutes established to study the need for forgiveness on personal, group, and global scales.[104]

On the international scene, the post-apartheid South African government, under the inspiration of Bishop Desmond Tutu, established the Truth and Reconciliation Commission in 2003. This Commission was charged with a courageous and creative mission – to address the gross violations of human rights committed on all sides of the previous conflict in order to bring about a peaceful community.[105] The Commission was charged with granting amnesty for political crimes, investigating past human rights violations, and offering reparations to the victims. In order to rebuild the country, a forum was needed to facilitate "transitional justice." The Commission offered criminal and civil amnesty to those individuals who would make a full confession of their crimes. Glaser points out that amnesty suits the Commission's philosophical approach to justice; justice is achieved not by retribution but by the restoration of community. Healing communities, in this view, requires truth-telling, forgiveness, acceptance and trust.

Writing from the Northern Ireland perspective, Fr. Michael Hurley, a Jesuit author and keen promoter of peace, adds further light to the process of reconciliation on a societal scale as he reflects on *koinonia* (Greek for "community"). He writes,

> It will be generally agreed that reconciliation means the ending of an estrangement, the restoration of *shalom*, of communication and communion, of *koinonia* between individuals or groups who are no longer talking to each other, who have broken off relations and are at odds with each other ... But if reconciliation is the overcoming of estrangement, the problems which are the cause of this estrangement cannot be ignored ... no reconciliation is possible without justice ... and without repentance.[106]

On a national level, Canada has its own Truth and Reconciliation Commission. It was established to address the concerns of Aboriginal peoples who were forced to attend residential schools during the nineteenth and 20th centuries as a way of assimilating them into the white culture. The Commission's task is to negotiate compensation for harm suffered by Aboriginal students in these schools – instances of physical and sexual abuse as well as the cultural and intergenerational impacts of being separated from family and tribal values. There is a desire for all parties involved – Aboriginal people, the Canadian government, and churches, which ran many of the schools at the request of the government – that the process involve more than financial compensation, but encompass inner healing as well. National Chief Phil Fontaine of the Assembly of First Nations expressed this sentiment when, in 2004, he wrote: "For many survivors, compensation is only one part of the answer. What we further need is an approach that allows survivors, Elders, counsellors and communities to be involved in the healing process."[107]

In addition to the work of the Truth and Reconciliation Commission, Prime Minister Stephen Harper made a public statement of apology on June 11, 2008, in the House of Commons on behalf of the federal government and all Canadians to former students of Indian residential schools. It is hoped that this public act will be another decisive step in the journey of all involved towards healing and reconciliation. Commenting on this event, the Honorable Chuck Strahl, Minister of Indian Affairs, said, "I am hopeful that the apology will help turn the page from the sad legacy of Indian Residential Schools and open a new chapter – one that is founded on renewed hope, faith, mutual respect and trust."[108]

In the workplace, where forgiveness is often an issue, mediation is available in most companies to resolve serious differences of opinion and other forms of conflict. Some companies have their own mediators; others hire them on a contract basis. The emotionally toxic effects of unresolved anger, resentment, the desire for revenge, the "silent treatment," and even hatred can severely pollute a work environment. Perhaps you have experienced the harmful effects of this kind of emotional upheaval where you work. Reasons for this behaviour vary, but here are some: someone spoke critically of you behind your back; a supervisor stole your ideas and presented them as his or her own; you received an unexpected pay cut; someone less qualified than you got the job you were expecting; or you lost your job due to downsizing at the company. These kinds of unpleasant experiences take their toll on us, both emotionally and spiritually. How to respond?

Here are the reflections of some practitioners. The first is from Robert Spitzer, S.J.

Forgiveness is perhaps the most difficult of all virtues because it seeks to temper vengeance, and vengeance always seems justifiable ... vengeance not only undermines family life, it can undermine organizational life and turn relatively peaceful environments into armed political camps ... forgiveness is a subset of humility. It is detachment from the hurt caused by intentional unfairness.[109]

Writer and inspirational speaker, Frederick Buechner says,

To forgive somebody is to say one way or another, "You have done something unspeakable, and by all rights I should call it quits between us. Both my pride and my principles demand no less.

However, although I make no guarantees that I will be able to forget what you've done and though we may both carry the scars for life, I refuse to let it stand between us. I still want you for my friend."[110]

On the other hand, sometimes the injury inflicted is unintentional. Lewis Smedes explains, "Forgiveness is God's invention for coming to terms with a world in which, despite their best intentions, people are unfair to each other and hurt each other deeply. He began by forgiving us. And he invites us all to forgive each other."[111] What can get in the way of this process is our pride. Sometimes this vice comes at us in sneaky ways, as Henri Nouwen explains.

I am struck by how I cling to my own wounded self. Why do I think so much about the people who have offended or hurt me?

Why do I allow them to have so much power over my feelings and emotions? Why can't I be simply grateful for the good they have done and forget about their failures and mistakes? It seems that in order to find my place in life I need to be angry, resentful, or hurt.

It even seems that these people give me my identity by the very ways in which they wounded me. Part of me is "the wounded one." It is hard to know who I am when I can no longer point my finger at someone who is the cause of my pain![112]

Joseph, the son of Jacob, experienced a whole range of emotions in the process of finally forgiving members of his own family who had betrayed him. The story is found in the Book of Genesis, chapters 37 to 45. Perhaps you will find yourself somewhere in Joseph's story. Sometimes I use this story in my retreats. When I do so, this is how I tell it:

Jacob had many sons, but he loved Joseph the best, because Joseph was the son of his old age. This favouritism resulted in jealousy among the brothers towards Joseph. The situation was exacerbated when Joseph told his brothers about his dreams. In one, he told them, he was in a field with his brothers tying up sheaves of wheat. He said to them, "Suddenly, my sheaf rose and stood upright; then your sheaves gathered around it, and bowed down to my sheaf" (37:7). This only fuelled the resentment of the brothers, and eventually led to their hating Joseph.

One day, his father sent Joseph to join his brothers, who were tending their father's flocks a fair distance from home. Joseph was seventeen at the time. The brothers noticed him from a distance, and seeing an opportunity, they plotted to kill him. They said to one another, "Here comes this dreamer. Come now, let us kill him and throw him into one of the pits (a dry well); then we shall say that a wild animal has devoured him, and we shall see what will become of his dreams" (37:19). One of the brothers, Reuben, had second thoughts, however, and convinced the others not to kill him outright but to throw him into a dry well. His purpose was to come back later, rescue Joseph and return him to their father. And so the brothers grabbed Joseph and tossed him into the well. We can imagine the terror that must have gripped Joseph and the terrible sense of betrayal by his own kin. As the brothers sat down by the well to eat, they saw a caravan heading toward Egypt. They decided to sell Joseph to the people in the caravan. When the caravan arrived in Egypt, those in charge sold Joseph to an employee of Pharaoh.

Years passed. Joseph got on well with the household of his Egyptian master. There were difficulties now and then, but for the purpose of this account we won't consider these now (they are in chapter 39, for the interested reader). What concerns us is that, when Joseph was 30, Pharaoh put him in charge of the whole land of Egypt. During the following seven years of plenty, when the land produced abundant crops, Joseph wisely collected and stored an immeasurable amount of grain in the storage areas. When this seven years of abundance came to an end, seven years of famine set in.

As the famine lengthened, it even affected the Jewish people. Jacob, Joseph's father, who had not seen his son for many years, and who thought Joseph had been killed and eaten by wild beasts, sent ten of his eleven remaining sons down to Egypt to buy an emergency supply of grain. Only Benjamin, the youngest son, stayed at home.

Now, here comes the interesting part. It was Joseph, as governor of the country, who had the responsibility of dispensing rations of grain to all the people. When his brothers arrived in the city, they were directed to Joseph. Coming into his presence, they knelt down before him with their faces to the ground. They did not realize that the man before them was their brother. Joseph, however, recognized them as soon as he saw them.

In terms of the virtue of forgiveness, what did he do? Did he immediately tell them who he was and seek reconciliation? No! Rather, he concealed his identity from them and spoke sternly to them. He asked where they had come from. He accused them of being spies. The brothers were dismayed and quickly responded that they had come only for food. They told Joseph about their home in the land of Canaan, that they came from a large family and that their youngest brother had stayed behind to be with their father. But Joseph, no doubt still suffering from what they had done to him when he was seventeen – and, one would hope, as an adult, more aware of how he had contributed to their negative attitude towards him by his boasting about the images in his dreams – decided to put them to a test. He demanded that they send one of their number back to their homeland and bring their youngest brother to him. Then he had them locked up in the guardhouse for three days. Before they were to leave, he said, they could all go but one.

During this time, Joseph was on an emotional roller coaster: he was stern with his brothers, but he also wept out of their sight. He remembered his father and the home that had been stolen from him while at the same time he found his life in Egypt satisfying. In terms of the healing journey of forgiveness, his responses were quite human (our response would not likely be so drastic as to put the other in jail, though we might imagine that possibility!). The process he went through shows us that we can't short-circuit forgiveness. We may have to go through a whole range of emotions to reach the point where we can let go of the resentment we feel towards those who have acted harshly against us and seek reconciliation.

The "coming together" did finally happen for Joseph and his brothers.

The brothers returned to Egypt with Benjamin, and went before Joseph to prove their trustworthiness. Here is the account from Genesis:

Then Joseph could no longer control himself before all those who stood by him, and he cried out, "Send everyone away from me." So no one stayed with him when Joseph made himself known to his brothers. And he wept so loudly that the Egyptians heard it, and the household of Pharaoh heard it. Joseph said to his brothers, "I am Joseph. Is my father still alive?" But his brothers could not answer him, so dismayed were they at his presence. Then Joseph said to his brothers, "Come closer to me." And they came closer.

He said, "I am your brother, Joseph, whom you sold into Egypt. And now do not be distressed, or angry with yourselves, because you sold me here; for God sent me before you to preserve life." ... Then he fell upon his brother Benjamin's neck and wept, while Benjamin wept upon his neck. And he kissed all his brothers and wept upon them; and after that his brothers talked with him. (Genesis 45:1-5, 14-15)

Two important insights in this story can help us on our own journey. First, we must take responsibility for our role in an estrangement if we have contributed to the disunity. This requires a certain amount of humility, a willingness to do some self-reflection, and courage. Courage is needed to face our dark side. As we saw in Joseph's story, he bears some responsibility for the depth of his brothers' negative attitude towards him. Perhaps it was this realization that eventually allowed him to forgive and embrace his brothers.

Second, it is important to remember how many times we have received God's mercy and forgiveness. Joseph came to this realization only as an adult, as we see in his speech to his brothers when he disclosed his identity to them. In the New Testament story of the Last Supper, after washing the disciples' feet, Jesus says, "Go and do likewise." In other words, as He has done for us we are to do to one another.

Pope John Paul II is a contemporary example of how to forgive another graciously. He visited the prison where the man who tried to assassinate him was held, and offered the man forgiveness. Pope John Paul II shared wise words in his 2002 Message for World Peace Day that can be applied on both personal and communal levels.

Forgiveness is above all a personal choice, a decision of the heart to go against the natural instinct to pay back evil with evil.

The measure of such a decision is the love of God, who draws us to himself in spite of our sin ... Forgiveness, therefore, has a divine source and criterion ... Forgiveness may seem like weakness, but it demands great spiritual strength and moral courage, both in granting it and in accepting it. It may seem in some way to diminish us, but in fact it leads us to a fuller and richer humanity, more radiant with the splendour of the Creator.[113]

7

Blessed are those who are generous; for they shall receive an eternal reward

The one who sows sparingly will also reap sparingly,
and the one who sows bountifully will also reap bountifully.
Each of you must give as you have made up your mind,
not reluctantly or under compulsion,
for God loves a cheerful giver.
—2 Corinthians 9:6-7

In striving to live a virtuous life, one source from which we draw inspiration is the Bible. As God deals with us, we learn in those sacred pages, we are to deal with one another. "For God so loved the world," John's Gospel says, "that he gave his only Son, so that everyone who believes in him may not perish but may have eternal life" (John 3:16).

This is the pinnacle of generosity.

We are challenged and encouraged in the sacred scriptures to be generous in our love and compassion – both to other human beings and to all of creation; to be lavish in our mercy and forgiveness, as the father of his wayward son was (Luke 15); and in the words of the Golden Rule, "to treat others as we wish to be treated."

Consider forgiveness, for example. We saw in the previous chapter that one aspect of this virtue is letting go – of hurt, of hate, of resentment, of pride, even of finding our identity in our "wounded self." In letting go, we offer to ourselves and to the other person two great gifts of generosity: mercy and the possibility of reconciliation.

According to the dictionary, the generous person is noble-minded, magnanimous, unselfish, great-hearted, and willing to share. In Steven Covey's terms, generosity comes from an "abundance mentality," or, as my friend Barry Giovanetto, a businessman, likes to say, "an attitude of abundance." Contrast these descriptive words with the opposite of generous: stingy, miserly, selfish, small of heart, covetous, and greedy.

Robert Roberts, in a masterful article called "Just a Little More: Greed and the Malling of Our Souls," offers the following explanation for why we embrace such negative qualities:

> There is a difference in self-concept between the greedy and the generous person. The self-concept of a greedy person is very tied up with her [or his] possessions, which make her feel secure. Such a person sees herself as weak or vulnerable to the extent that she is short of possessions, and strong and secure if she has them.
>
> The generous person, by contrast, does not think of herself as built up or secured by what she possesses. Her security and her substance come from elsewhere, so she can give away her material goods and do so cheerfully.[114]

The "elsewhere" that Roberts refers to is God. Generous people trust in the Creator for their security. They find their substance as persons, their integrity, and their inner strength precisely in those acts of sharing their possessions.

I am reminded here of the "Principle and Foundation" meditation (described in Chapter 1) in the Spiritual Exercises of St. Ignatius of Loyola, especially the part dealing with "inordinate attachments" – obstacles within us that keep us from doing what God asks of us. As Professor André Comte-Sponville of the Sorbonne in Paris says, "We can only give what we possess and only on condition of not being possessed by what we own."[115]

The Parable of the Good Samaritan (Luke 10) illustrates the main characteristics of the virtue of generosity. Lest we think that being generous only has to do with providing financial help to someone in need, Jesus points out that first the Samaritan expands our concept of who our neighbour is. The Samaritan is not moved to compassion at the sight of a fellow Samaritan but of a Jew. As we have seen in previous chapters, Jews and Samaritans in the time of Jesus disliked and avoided contact with one another. Second, the Samaritan offers more than a charitable donation of money. He takes time out of his schedule to approach the victim to check on his injuries. Seeing that the man is in dire straits, he pours oil and wine from his own containers on the man's wounds. Then he bandages the wounds. Next he lifts the man onto his own animal and takes him to a nearby inn, where he cares for him. The following day, he gives the innkeeper two silver coins, instructing him to take care of the wounded man. The Samaritan extends his generosity even further by telling the innkeeper that, on his way back to Jerusalem from Jericho, he will stop by the inn and pay any additional expenses the innkeeper may incur in helping the victim recover. The Samaritan thus gives of his time, his energy, his concern, and his goods, as well as his money. There is no indication that he acts grudgingly. This is noble-minded behaviour – unselfish and unself-conscious liberality of the heart. Jesus challenges our perspective on sharing in this parable. Writer Carlos Bravo says, "Jesus turns human values upside down – the central thing is not to accumulate and to *have*, but to *share*."[116]

Generosity manifests in many forms. Later in this chapter we will look at some of the most obvious ones, such as volunteerism and philanthropy. For now, let us consider some unexpected appearances of this virtue.

I used to minister part-time in a parish in the hills of Tijuana, Mexico. The people in the neighbourhood were economically poor but rich in hospitality. Occasionally, I would take friends from the United States with me to meet them. One Saturday afternoon, some friends I have known since high school drove south from Los Angeles and accompanied me to Colonia (District) Esperanza (which means "hope"), where the church is located. A fiesta for the children was being held in the playground next to the church; we were invited to join in. As we got out of our car and headed toward the wire fence surrounding the party area, one of the children came to meet us from the other side of the fence. She called out to us, and one of my friends from the other side of the border walked over to greet her (he told me later he thought she was going to ask him for money and he was prepared to give her some change). As he reached the fence, she thrust her hand through an opening. In her palm was an orange. She gave it to my friend with a smile on her face and cheerfully said, "Buenos dias!" My friend was stunned. Here he was, a successful lawyer and Christian from Los Angeles, and a child with very little of monetary value was showing him what true generosity is all about. He has never forgotten the little girl's gesture, even though the event took place over fifteen years ago.

Twice in the past 25 years, I have made difficult moves to new locations. Both times, the virtue of generosity played a significant role. My first move happened when I was asked to leave what I considered the closest place to heaven – the San Francisco Bay Area. I had lived there for twelve years in a large Jesuit community, with family and other close friends nearby. I was being asked to move to a city at the other end of the state, where there were few Jesuits and where I knew hardly anyone. Furthermore, I would be living in a very poor section of the city, economically speaking. I struggled with this possible move for some time.

One day, I was meditating on the parable of the rich young man (Matthew 19:16-30). In the story, the young man asked Jesus what good he must do to gain eternal life. Jesus responded that if the man wanted to live his faith more fully, he should go sell what he had and give the money to the poor. As I reflected on this situation of the young man and Jesus, I thought about my own dilemma. I asked myself, in relation to moving to the other city, "What do I have and what can I give?" What I *had* at the time was the security of living in a place that was not only geographically beautiful but that offered an abundance of communal support. Both of these factors were difficult to let go of. To the question "What do I have to *give?*" the answer was simple and profound: my time and my love. As a result of this meditation, I was able to make the move without regrets.

Perhaps you have had a similar experience of being asked to let go of something precious (though not in monetary terms) to follow God's invitation. If so, you have discovered, as I did, that the most difficult things to let go of are not financial, but personal.

After living in the location mentioned above for sixteen years, I was asked once again to make a move. This time, it was to another country – Canada – and not to a city, but to a First Nations Reserve (Indian Reservation) in rural Alberta. I had never lived among Aboriginal people before, and had always been a city dweller. In addition, on the Reserve I would be living alone on a prairie over an hour's drive from the city of Calgary. Fortunately, I had stayed at the Reserve for two weeks the previous summer, so I had met some of the people. I had also given some retreats in Calgary over the previous four years, and now had friends in the city. However, there was only one other Jesuit in southern Alberta, and he was close to retirement. While I was on my annual eight-day retreat that year, I realized I was in dire need of two particular virtues if I was going to be able to make the move – generosity and courage. The challenge was to be of "noble mind," to be "great of heart." In prayer, I put my needs in God's hands, acknowledging my fears and reluctance. My prayers were heard. I was given what I needed. Two months later, I left California for rural Alberta.

Generosity is the virtue of giving and sharing. It is the opposite of selfishness, as magnanimity is the opposite of pettiness, and greatness of heart is the opposite of smallness of spirit. Two philosophers who contributed much to the understanding of the virtue of generosity were René Descartes and Benedict de Spinoza. Descartes emphasized the role of freedom in handling our emotions: an awareness that we are free to act with good intentions, and do, in fact, act. On the virtue of generosity, he wrote, "To be generous is to be able to will and hence to give, when so many others seem to know only how to desire, to demand, to take."[117] Spinoza suggested that a person develop a "morality of generosity" so that our actions come spontaneously from the heart.[118] We can act generously from a variety of motives, positive or negative: sincerely and with love; out of a sense of justice; from a position of obligation or duty; out of compassion; out of guilt; or to impress others. André Comte-Sponville writes, "[True] generosity elevates us *towards others*, as it were, and toward ourselves as beings freed from the pettiness that is the self."[119] By "self" he means that part of ourselves that is motivated in base desires. We are free to act generously, as we saw earlier, insofar as we are not possessively tied to what we have, for possessiveness limits our freedom.

Consider the following two examples of generous living. One is from the Bible, the other from modern times. The biblical story, known as "the widow's mite," takes place at the Temple in Jerusalem. Jesus is there with some of his disciples.

> Jesus sat down opposite the treasury, and watched the crowd putting their money into the treasury. Many rich people put in large sums. A poor widow came and put in two small copper coins, which are worth a penny. Then he called his disciples and said to them, "Truly I tell you, this poor widow has put in more than all those who are contributing to the treasury. For all of them have contributed out of their abundance; but she out of her poverty has put in everything she had, all she had to live on." (Mark 12:41-44)

Let's take a closer look at the passage and its implications for us. First, this incident is directly connected with the passage that comes just before it, where Jesus denounced those scribes who exploited widows. Scribes in Jesus' day were the scholars and intellectuals of Judaism who received the title "rabbi." Some were unscrupulous; they abused their religious position, especially towards poor widows and poor people in general. They were, in Descartes' words, "takers." Second, Jesus is not suggesting that we put ourselves into the poorhouse with our generosity. St. Paul addresses this very point in his Second Letter to the Corinthians where he writes, "The relief of others ought not to impoverish you" (8:12-14, NAB). Descartes also has something to say about the need for balance in giving: "Those who are generous in this way [that is, freely] are naturally led to do great deeds, and at the same time not to undertake anything of which they do not feel themselves capable."[120] Jesus is speaking about giving from our substance and not just from our surplus. The widow, by her simple offering, teaches us about being detached from material possessions; the Samaritan did the same when he gave of his time, his care, *and* his financial help.

The second example is not as radical as the widow in the Bible story, but its effect on me was significant. This series of events occurred over an entire year at a Calgary restaurant and involved the most unusual waiter I have ever met. I call this story "Going the Extra Miles." I first met Tony when I went to the restaurant where he works. I had won a $50 gift certificate to this eatery, so I took a friend with me for dinner. As our waiter, Tony was not only efficient, but also very kind and solicitous. When we commented, for example, on the excellence of the bread that came with the meal, he gave us a loaf to take home, with directions on how to bake it! When we told him we had decided to forgo having dessert (because it would have taken us over the $50), he brought us a large free dessert, with two forks. "On the house!" he told us. I was so taken by the quality of his service that the following day I wrote a letter to the manager, telling him how pleased my companion and I were with his establishment, with special emphasis on our experience of Tony. A week later, I received a thank you from the administrative office of the restaurant. In gratitude for my affirming letter (evidently, restaurants get more negative letters than positive ones), the manager sent me an additional gift certificate, this one for $25. The next time I went to the restaurant, I asked to be in Tony's section. Every time I returned for lunch or dinner, I asked for him, and so we gradually got to know one another. Each time I went, he would surprise me with some new generous act. One time on my day off, I went to the restaurant for lunch by myself. I brought a novel with me to pass the time. Tony asked if I wanted to read the local newspaper. I declined, telling him I preferred the national one. Ten minutes later he returned with the national paper; he had gone across the street to a buy it for me! Tony's kindness and generosity seemed boundless. I learned a lot from him about service and about the positive effect that even small acts of generosity can have on someone.

St. Matthias Anglican Church in Guelph, Ontario, sent the following "gift list" on generous living to its parishioners as a reflection for Christmas. I think it sums up what a morality of generosity is all about.

- The Gift of Time – Just "being" with someone can be a great comfort to them.
- The Gift of a Good Example – Most people learn fundamental attitudes and behaviours by observing other people.
- The Gift of Acceptance – People begin to change when they know they are accepted for who they are.
- The Gift of Seeing the Best in People – When we expect others to respond in a positive way, they usually come through for us.
- The Gift of Privacy – Too often we tend to "smother" other people with questions and demands on their time.

- The Gift of Self-Esteem – Criticism [that is not construc-
  tive] stunts growth. Encouragement and recognition help
  a person to blossom.
- The Gift of Giving up a Bad Habit – We display love for
  our self and for others when we give up activities that are
  hurtful or unhealthy.
- The Gift of Self-Disclosure – Bottling up feelings and
  resentments deprives the other person of truly knowing
  who we are.
- The Gift of Helping Someone Learn Something New –
  Helping someone learn something new is an important
  investment in their future happiness.
- The Gift of Really Listening – Few of us know how to
  listen in an effective manner – give it a try for someone!
- The Gift of Fun – It's important when we can help those
  close to us to find fun in ordinary small events.
- The Gift of Letting Others Give to Us – When we let
  others give to us, and when we are able to accept their
  gifts in a gracious and mature manner, we may be giving
  them one of the most important gifts of all.[121]

The Gift of Volunteerism

The city of Calgary, Alberta, prides itself on its volunteerism. This was especially true in the preparation and running of
the 1988 Winter Olympics. People from all walks of life turned
out to help make the event a successful one. This outpouring of
generosity is not surprising in a city that draws half its popula-
tion from the rural areas of Canada. These seekers come to the
city with values of collaboration and co-operation that served
them well in farming and ranching communities.

Volunteerism has different connotations, depending on
one's country or culture. Project Kaleidoscope of the Volunteer
Centre of Calgary published the following overview on the act
of volunteering. It is instructive to see the differences of under-

standing and valuation of this aspect of generosity. It is especially helpful to know the differences, since many recent immigrants from the communities listed below now live in the large cities of North America.

- China – Older Chinese see volunteering as a courtesy and an obligation to the community. They prefer the term "giving a helping hand" to "volunteering" because volunteering is associated with social work. Younger Chinese volunteer to gain vital work experience and to have fun.
- Philippines – Filipinos interpret the word "volunteer" to mean community spirit or community involvement. Volunteering is an informal activity built on trust and friendship.
- Ismaili Muslim – Ismaili Muslims experience volunteering as a religious requirement and therefore it is a part of daily living. As a community, every Ismaili Muslim is involved in volunteering.
- Latin America – Latin American people see volunteering as something privileged people do. Volunteering is perceived, especially by recent immigrants, as an indication of class. Volunteering is generally seen as a private value and not an activity to be advertised on a resume.
- Ecuador – The word *voluntario* was introduced to Latin America by the Spanish. It often refers to foreign volunteers. Ecuadorians today prefer *compañero*, meaning someone to break bread with. A long tradition of Christian charity and the desire to serve God motivates Ecuadorians to volunteer today.
- Poland – Polish immigrants come from a country where many were forced to volunteer as a way of promoting government ideology. Therefore, there may be a negative attitude towards volunteering, particularly among recent immigrants. Many older established community members volunteer with the Polish community.

- Sikh – The Sikh community translates volunteering to mean "service," their third religious commandment. In India, Sikhs engage in community volunteer work as a part of daily life.
- Japan – In Japan, the concept of volunteering is not well known. Volunteer activities must be congruent with the needs of the group. Motivation to volunteer is often connected to a sense of obligation: people who received help feel obliged to repay it with their labour and time.
- Australia – In Australia, the term "volunteering" has certain historical, sociological, and class connotations, and is overtly or implicitly disparaging. By contrast, expressions such as "community involvement" and "lending a hand" are positive terms.
- Germany – In Germany, *ehrenamtliche* is the term most often used to refer to volunteers. The word, which means "honorary position," carries connotations of duty and formally held offices. Many volunteers prefer to describe their work than to identify themselves as *ehrenamtliche*.[122]

People in North America find outlets to help others in a wide variety of ways. I see many examples of this in my life. For instance, two of my business friends in Calgary volunteer their time as coaches, one for his daughter's soccer team, the other for a junior football squad. Another friend, who is a university professor in philosophy, freely shared his expertise in ethics over a six-week period to a class composed of street people. A lawyer who attends the parish where I lived regularly takes on cases pro bono. Another person I have come to know and admire is Jim Pender, a clinical social worker. When I asked him about how he tries to live the virtue of generosity, he replied, "I always try to see a few clients for free. Underlying this is my own experience that I am not so very different from any of my clients – we are all wounded in our own respective ways. I also try to mentor younger colleagues or those who are just beginning in the profession."

Many churches in Calgary, as in other cities, provide temporary overnight shelter, meals, and fellowship to homeless families and individuals. This program, known as Inn from the Cold, depends on the generosity of volunteers to set up the sleeping area, prepare the meals, play cards or games with the adults and the children, and help with cleanup. In addition to this program, churches and other religious institutions offer a hot meal for both the working poor and people who are homeless; the churches, too, depend on the kindness of volunteers, many of whom come from the business community.

Writer Jean Maalouf suggests that there is an intimate connection between generosity and kindness.[123] Even the simple things we do for another – a genuine smile, a warm word, a listening ear, a helping hand – are real blessings. They may heal a person's deepest fears of isolation and loneliness. One of my acquaintances in Calgary has a unique ministry of kindness; he walks the alleys in the downtown core and chats with those who make their meagre living collecting bottles and cans from dumpsters and other trash containers. I asked him one time what I might carry with me on my downtown walks that would be appropriate to give to street people (the social agencies prefer people not to give money, which leaves the person asking in a position of dependency). He suggested four items – power bars (not candy), beef jerky, tobacco and cigarette papers, and bus tickets. And, of course, to give these items in a kindly manner.

Assisting people who are down on their luck is all in a day's work for David Ransom Jr., owner of D&R Press in Chicago. Writer Ann Meyer explains:

> He is not afraid to hire those who most need a lucky break. He has pulled employees out of bars and sobered them up. He let one who had no place to stay sleep under a table in his print shop. He paid for an attorney to get another out of jail.

And he has offered restaurant vouchers to a worker who was overextended on credit card bills. "It's my upbringing," said Ransom, who describes himself as a born-again Christian. "I can't see someone starving in this country."[124]

As a priest I am aware of the profound impact of a simple act of kindness. This is especially true for those who are grieving the death of someone they love dearly. As a human being, I am also painfully aware of the selfishness that sometimes creeps into my heart and tries to waylay a good deed. Thanks be to God, who knows me better than I know myself! This gracious God has helped me on more than one occasion get past my selfishness. Such was the case one Christmas season. It was late in the afternoon on December 21. Like everyone else, I was trying my best to buy gifts for friends as well as wrap the gifts. In addition, I had a lot of paperwork to finish before the end of the year. In the midst of this busyness, the phone rang. One of our parishioners was in the hospital, dying. He had specifically asked his family to call me for anointing. My initial reaction was not what you would call a holy one. I was tired. There was snow on the ground, and it was very cold outside. I didn't favour getting into my winter gear, driving to the hospital about 20 minutes away, and searching for a parking place in sub-zero weather. But go I did, thanks to God's grace. As a result of this sacrifice, I was able to help a dying man go peacefully to his Creator and was warmly embraced by his family. I hadn't known that he and his wife (who predeceased him) had ten children, now adults. Six of them live in or near Calgary. They and their families are now among my closest friends. They have invited me to their homes, taken me out for breakfast after Sunday Mass, and, by their kindness, inspired me to be a more giving person.

Educating our youth to be men and women of loving-kindness to those in need is the goal of high schools that require a certain number of hours of volunteer service as an integral part of the curriculum. Large cities offer volunteer programs for college graduates and people with other life skills to serve for a year or more, those who are economically poor in Canada, the United States, and Third World countries. Associations such as the Rotary Club, the Knights of Columbus, and Big Sisters/Big Brothers consider volunteering to be an essential part of their charters. Add to these excellent efforts those volunteers who give of their time and energy on behalf of organizations that promote social justice and world peace, such as the Jesuit Volunteer Corps and the Peace Corps. In Chapter 5 we considered ways to better the environment. There are many people with a deep sensitivity to the challenges facing our planet. Whether it's recycling, replanting, or renewing our natural resources, volunteers are the lifeblood of the worldwide effort to save us from ourselves. Emily Dickinson expressed sensitivity to people and to nature in a symbolic way:

> If I can stop one heart from breaking,
> I shall not live in vain;
> If I can ease one life the aching
> or cool one pain,
> or help one fainting robin
> unto his nest again,
> I shall not live in vain.[125]

In the article "Virtual Volunteers Fill the Digital Void," the author explains that a "virtual volunteer" is someone who carries out his or her volunteer activities with little or no direct contact with the recipient.[126] They are part of a growing trend, particularly among Information Technology professionals – website designers, database managers, computer specialists, etc. – who prefer to conduct their volunteer efforts from their homes, home offices, or offices. where they have access to all the technology they need. Some of these men and women freely offer their assistance to non-profit agencies that may not have sufficient technological resources on site. Others act as "e-mentors" through a secure website for children who need tutoring or mentoring.

Big Brothers/Big Sisters runs the program. According to the article, a positive relationship develops between the tutor and the student that benefits both, since, even with computers, there is back-and-forth communication. A willingness to share one's expertise and experience is one of the hallmarks of the virtue of generosity. As the ancient sage Confucius wrote,

> A [person] of humanity is one who,
> in seeking to establish [herself],
> finds a foothold for others
> and who, desiring attainment for [herself],
> helps others to attain.[127]

Philanthropy

We are, in the words of one observer, entering into the "golden age of philanthropy" through the extraordinary generosity of people such as Bill and Melinda Gates and Warren Buffet.

The Gates family has contributed $30 billion to its foundation; Buffet has given $31 billion to his. These donations are being put to work primarily to reduce poverty, disease, and premature death in the developing world. The website of the Gates Foundation, under "Our Values," states, "All lives – no matter where they are being led – have equal value."

The dictionary defines philanthropy as practical benevolence, especially on a large scale, to increase the well-being of humankind. Certainly Bill and Melinda Gates and Warren Buffet are fulfilling the essence of this definition. The same is true of those with fewer financial resources who pool their money to try to improve the lot of their fellow human beings and the planet itself.

For Aristotle, generosity (and thus philanthropy) consists in giving the right amount to the right people at the right time and in the right way. Aristotle was a realist. He suggested that it is necessary to practise this virtue with humility, because the actual practice of generosity invariably falls short due to our human weakness.[128] Warren Buffet adds a note of his own to this humble stance when he admits that society is responsible for much of his wealth – along with, as some of my successful business friends put it, a lot of luck.

As in volunteerism, there are a variety of possible motivations for sharing one's goods. However, motivation is not a big concern for those who are in desperate financial need; they are just happy to have food on the table and other basic needs met. Whatever their ultimate motivation, I admire Bill and Melinda Gates and Warren Buffet. The Gates Foundation website also contains this statement: "From everyone to whom much has been given, much will be required" (Luke 12:48).

These philanthropists seem to have their act together. Perhaps they have also read some of the words of St. Paul and St. John. St. Paul has a way of writing about challenging concepts courageously. In his First Letter to Timothy, he proclaims,

> As for those who in the present age are rich, command them not to be haughty, or to set their hopes on the uncertainty of riches, but rather on God who richly provides us with everything for our enjoyment. They are to do good, to be rich in good works, generous, ready to share, thus storing up for themselves the treasure of a good foundation for the future, so that they may take hold of the life that really is life. (6:17-19)

In this way, St. Paul situates riches in a broader context than the here and now. He points us towards God in our emotional and spiritual detachment from riches. St. John, meanwhile, gives us the "horizontal" – here and now – view by asking a penetrating question: "How does God's love abide in anyone who has the world's goods and sees a brother or sister in need and yet refuses to help?" (1 John 3:17).

Both perspectives are needed for a balanced approach to philanthropic efforts. After all, millions of people are in desperate need of the basic goods of life – food, clothing, decent housing, medical care, opportunities for a good education, and meaningful work. Philanthropy is another dimension of "Love your neighbour as yourself."

Each of us, regardless of how much money we have, can offer some of our resources to those who have less than we do. Nothing is too little in God's eyes, as the story of the widow's mite reveals. Fundraisers for non-profit organizations are well aware of the important contribution of donors who are unable to give large sums but give what they can on a regular basis.

Consider the following individuals who have made or are making a difference in people's lives by their generous actions.

Fran, a campus minister at Duquesne University in Pittsburgh shares the following recollection about her father:

> My father worked hard, developing a fledgling milk business into a successful operation that not only provided milk for our small town, but also good, well-paid work for his employees and a place for my siblings and me to learn ethical business practices. Although he did not need partners in the business, after World War II he offered partnerships to one of his brothers and a brother-in-law so that these young men returning from the war would have stable employment. He treated his employees with respect and kindness, while calling them to an honest day's work. He enjoyed talking with his customers and being an active, vital member of the community. *He often forgave debts for people with families who could not pay their milk bills while continuing to deliver milk to them anyway.* In those pre-civil rights days, he made no distinction between people of different races or ethnic background ... these were simply a part of my father's way of being.[129]

Jon Talty, president of OKW Architects in Chicago, found a way to be philanthropic within his company. He once gave a young associate a $4,000 advance on his year-end bonus because the associate needed the money to buy a house. The young man hadn't approached Talty for the money, but when Talty asked how the house hunt was going and learned of the young man's disappointment at being short a few thousand dollars, he found a way to help him out. "I told him, 'I'll give you the money right now,'" Talty said. The man was thrilled, but more than that, the act of kindness conveyed the firm's confidence in the associate, Talty recalled. [130]

In the small parish I served in Tijuana, Mexico, some of our parishioners had green cards so they could work in San Diego, California. Since the wages are much greater on the United States side of the border, most improvements to the houses of these men and women would come from money earned in the US. These workers also provided financial help to their extended families. In addition, their income benefited the whole parish. Similarly, workers from El Salvador who have jobs in the US send home money to their families. In fact, this is the largest source of income for some countries. The practices of these workers in Tijuana and El Salvador are examples of "practical benevolence" and thus are philanthropic activities.

In conducting the research for the theme of donations, I came across the Jewish philosopher Maimonides. This sage, who lived in the twelfth century, was an expert in Jewish law. He organized the tradition's many insights and directives into a graded hierarchy of *Tzedakah* (charity), from the most sublime to the barely acceptable, taking into account the effects on recipient and donor alike. I was led to Maimonides' "Eight Degrees of Charity" by my good friend Ted Valentine, a retired businessman. Maimonides lists the Eight in reverse order, from the least honourable to the most honourable.

8. When donations are given grudgingly.

7. When one gives less than he should, but does so cheerfully.

6. When one gives directly to the poor upon being asked.

5. When one gives directly to the poor without being asked.

4. When the recipient is aware of the donor's identity, but the donor does not know the identity of the recipient.

3. When the donor is aware of the recipient's identity, but the recipient is unaware of the source.

2. When the donor and the recipient are unknown to each other.

1. The highest form of charity is to help sustain a person before they become impoverished by offering a substantial gift in a dignified manner, or by extending a suitable loan, or by helping them find employment or establish themselves in business so as to make it unnecessary for them to become dependent on others.[131]

In the Hindu tradition, The Bhagavad Gita, a religious poem in which God is seen in all things, presents this teaching on gift-giving:

The gift which is given without thought of recompense, in the belief that it ought to be made, in a fit place, at an opportune time and to a deserving person – such a gift is Pure.

That which is given for the sake of the results it will produce, or with the hope of recompense, or grudgingly – that may truly be said to be an outcome of passion. (Bhagavad Gita 17:20-21)

My friend Allan King, a mining engineer who has studied Buddhism extensively, pointed out to me that the Buddha believed in the power of even a small gift because of its ripple effect. A person of integrity gives a gift:

- with a sense of conviction
- attentively
- in season
- with an empathetic heart
- without adversely affecting himself or others.[132]

If your desire is to give to a charitable organization, you need to research the organization and its activities. Most of us are bombarded with invitations to donate money, especially during the holiday season. You want to be sure that the recipient has a genuine need. It is helpful to choose a cause that means something to you personally. University professor Bill Prior has this to say about donating to a charity, a church, or another social organization: "... the person performing the act of generosity says in effect, 'I want to support this worthy organization. I want to be part of an effort to make my community, and ultimately the world, a better place.'"[133]

Paul Schervish, Director of the Center on Wealth and Philanthropy at Boston College, has some interesting ideas on donating. For those who wish to use their wealth as a tool to achieve higher purposes, who want their donation to be used to positive effect, and who wish to hand on to their children the wisdom they have learned in giving, he suggests creating a "moral biography of wealth." This "biography" is a spiritual process of self-examination that goes well beyond portfolio analysis or financial tools, says Schervish. He explains,

> A moral biography [of wealth] is simply the way people conscientiously combine two essential elements in their daily lives: personal capacity – whether intellectual, creative or financial – and moral compass, defined as the array of purposes, aspirations and long-term goals to which they choose to devote that capacity ... that capacity has the potential to have a very positive impact, or a very harmful one.[134]

The first step to making wise choices with your wealth, according to Schervish, is to clarify your personal capacity to find out how financially secure you are – both "your resource stream now and in the future as well as clarifying the expenditure stream you desire for yourself and your progeny." Second, clarify your talents and interests. Third, ascertain what the goals are you wish to achieve for yourself, your family, and the world (moral compass).[135]

My friends Jim and Sally have been abundantly blessed financially. They are also very generous people who echo Schervish's three-step plan in sharing their resources.

> God has blessed Sally and me and our family. We believe that everything ultimately comes from God and that we have an obligation to share what we have with our global brothers and sisters in need. I like to build things and to make sure they are well maintained. So we choose places and projects where this is possible. Sally and I make it a point to visit these places and to get to know some of the people who will benefit from our investment. We believe that this is a vital component to our giving. The amazing thing is that we feel we are truly blessed by the people we meet.

> We find the person of Jesus Christ in them, which makes our donating a form of prayer as well as an action of generosity. We have four adult children who, thankfully, share our concern for others. Our hope is that our entire family will continue to be good stewards.

Why do a moral biography of wealth? Schervish elucidates:

> Sometimes wealth-holders are offered tools – trusts, foundations, insurance policies – before they really know just why they need them. By first clarifying with [their] financial advisor(s) the amount [they] have and the purpose [they] wish to use it for, from the outset, [they] can more effectively deploy the financial tools that are offered.[136]

What about their children? Schervish suggests that the best thing wealthy parents can do for their children is to have them discern their own moral biography as it unfolds; their children will then also be conscientious in the use of their financial assets.

I bring this chapter to a close with these integrative words by André Comte-Sponville.

... generosity, like all the other virtues, is multiple both in its content and in the names that we call it or that serve to describe it. Combined with courage, it turns out to be heroism. Joined by justice, it becomes equity.

Coupled with compassion, it becomes benevolence. In league with mercy, it becomes leniency. But its most beautiful name is its secret, an open secret that everyone knows: accompanied by gentleness, it is called kindness.[137]

8

Blessed are those who have the courage of their convictions; for they are modern heroes and heroines

I hereby command you: Be strong and courageous;
do not be frightened or dismayed, for the Lord your God
is with you wherever you go.
—*Joshua 1:9*

You must do the thing you think you cannot do.
—*Eleanor Roosevelt*

Courage is being scared to death, but saddling up anyway.
—*John Wayne*

Growing up in the peaceful 1950s in southern California, I didn't think of myself as especially courageous. I didn't like to fight. I was much more of a lover than a fighter. In college I went out for the boxing team, perhaps to prove to myself that I was brave after all. It was after I joined the Jesuits in my mid-20s that I discovered other, more profound ways of being a person of courage than using my fists. In the Jesuit Novitiate (the first two years of training), I determined to be the best priest I could be. I didn't know how much courage it would take to achieve that goal.

The first serious challenge came when I realized that I had a poor self-image and an inferiority complex. Before I became a Jesuit, I had put my sense of self-worth in things – a good job, a full social life, the car of my dreams – not in myself. In addition, I grew up with an authoritarian father, which caused me to feel inferior in certain situations. To face these "demons" in my personality, I needed courage, and lots of it. Fortunately, I had great mentors in the Jesuits. My first mentor, a priest wise in the ways of the spiritual journey, gave me a phrase to say every time I felt down about myself: "God loves me and nothing else matters." He also suggested I reflect on some passages from the Bible, such as Isaiah 43:4 ("You are precious in my eyes and glorious, and ... I love you"), Psalm 139:14 ("I praise you, for I am fearfully and wonderfully made. Wonderful are your works; that I know very well"), and, to help me persevere in reversing a lifetime of self-doubt, Isaiah 54:10 ("The mountains may depart and the hills be removed, but my steadfast love shall not depart from you, and my covenant of peace shall not be removed, says the Lord who has compassion on you"). I learned by experience that personal prayer helps us to transform our sense of identity beyond the roles we play, beyond what describes us, to a deeper dimension of selfhood.

Courage is about strength of character. It is the virtue we need to continue our quest to be a better moral person in the face of whatever obstacles lie within us – especially fear. Fear is a basic human emotion. Some fears can paralyze us emotionally. In both our personal and professional lives, we fear possible failure, change, making a mistake, intimacy, losing control, and the unknown. In the early 1980s, I was given a prayer to address fears. I call it "A Prayer for Inner Freedom" (see Appendix D for the steps involved in this prayer).[138] I have found this method of prayer very effective and have heard from many people of the benefits of using this spiritual technique to augment their personal efforts to get at the root of their fears.

We need the virtue of courage, then, to embark on and persist in the inner journey. In my experience, we also need to trust in the One Who knows us best and wants us to be fully alive. St. Augustine put it well when he wrote, "To the one who does what in him lies, God does not deny grace."[139]

The second inner challenge I faced was my anger. I had been with the Jesuits for five years when I experienced depression for the first time in my life. I sought the help of a counsellor, who helped me to see that repressed anger was the cause of the depression. I lived in an inner-city parish at the time. The pastor had an authoritarian personality like my father's. Through the guidance of the counsellor, I discovered that I had repressed the normal human emotion of anger since I was a child. At the core of this issue was my fear of rejection by my father, who would not allow us to express our anger when my siblings or I disagreed with him. The fear of rejection is the fear of losing the love we need from those we most admire, respect, and love through doing something that displeases them. With my identity now based in God's unconditional love for me and my new-found reservoir of courage as a Jesuit novice, I determined to face both my past (my father) and the present (the pastor) by going within again to confront this unhealthy aspect of my personality. I like very much Eleanor Roosevelt's insight into this process:

> You gain strength, courage and confidence by every experience in which you really stop to look at fear in the face. You are able to say to yourself, "I lived through this horror. I can take the next thing that comes along."[140]

I had reached the same conclusion that David Whyte describes in his brilliant book, *The Heart Aroused*, about our responsibility to go into our past in order to be healed for the present.

> You can blame your mother, you can blame your father ... for the problems with which you are destined to wrestle, but ultimately you are the one in whom they have made a home. You are the one who must say, *thus far and no farther*, and then go down and confront them yourself.[141]

My friend David Irvine, who has a background in counselling, pointed out to me that one of the roots of the word
"character" is "chisel."[142] A chisel is a tool used to strip away
waste material from an object in order to get down to what
is essential. God helps us to get to the core of who we are by
helping us chisel off the negative aspects of our personality in
order to make us more like Jesus. We can pray for the courage we
need to undergo this process, as the Jewish prophets did when
God asked them to speak challenging words to the people. The
prophets knew their weaknesses. They knew that without God's
help, they would not be able to get past their fears. We can ask
the Lord for assistance, as St. Peter did when he asked Jesus if
he could walk to him on the water. In calming the storm, Jesus
had said to the apostles, "Take heart, it is I; do not be afraid"
(Matthew 14:27).

Sometimes it feels as if we are walking on water as we face
our fears and head into the healing process. We can draw inner
strength from the Psalms. They offer support and comfort, as
we see in the following examples.

> I love you, O Lord, my strength.
> The Lord is my rock, my fortress and my deliverer,
> my God, my rock, in whom I take refuge,
> my shield and the horn of my salvation,
> my stronghold.
> (Psalm 18:1-3)

> The Lord is my light and my salvation—
> whom shall I fear?
> The Lord is the stronghold of my life;
> of whom shall I be afraid?
> (Psalm 27:1)

> In you, O Lord, I seek refuge;
> do not let me ever be put to shame;
> in your righteousness deliver me.
> Incline your ear to me;

rescue me speedily.
Be a rock of refuge for me,
a strong fortress to save me.
(Psalm 31:1-2, 5)

Business leaders, like all leaders, must face fears regularly and learn to get past them. In a talk to business leaders in Australia, spiritual teacher Andrew Cohen said this about being a genuine leader, something this Beatitude inspires us to be:

If we aspire to be an authentic leader we must always be willing to:

- Stand alone
- Live fearlessly
- Act heroically
- Want to be free and true more than anything else
- Take unconditional responsibility for oneself
- Face everything and avoid nothing
- Live for a higher purpose.[143]

Courage in the Workplace

Rosemary Radford Ruether, in an insightful article on courage as a Christian value, defines this virtue in the following way: It is the capacity and power of the will that makes a person strive for what is good and be willing to adhere to this commitment to virtue in the face of all opposition.[144]

Consider the following story, which I heard from a man who works in the petroleum industry. It is a testimony to integrity and courage.

I am a petroleum landman by profession. I work for oil and natural gas companies and am responsible for the acquisition and disposition of mineral rights that are acquired by these companies. The industry is very competitive.

In Alberta, Canada, where I live and work, the Crown [government] land is sold at provincial land sales every two weeks. The bids are closed, which means anyone interested in purchasing a particular parcel of land submits their individual bids. The government only publishes the winning bid. When a new oil or natural gas "discovery" is made, the company involved tries its best to keep this information secret so they can purchase as much of the surrounding land as possible to enhance the drilling site.

A while ago, I was a participant in a group of four companies whose representatives gathered together to pool their knowledge and money in order to try to purchase a large piece of land where a major new discovery was expected.

Each of the four companies was large, with a lot of cash at their disposal. The date of the sale was quickly approaching. Rumours were flying that this was to be a big money maker for whoever secured the bid. The pressure was on all four of these companies to get a piece of the action. As a sale approaches, each landman's job is to represent to the other landmen (three others, in this case) the maximum amount of money his or her company is prepared to pay for the land. The company that I was representing was in the final stage of considering how much money to invest in the sale. It was then that a moral challenge presented itself to me. One of the other landmen, a man quite a bit older than myself, approached me privately and said, "I don't really like these other companies. Now that we have all the financial information on what they plan to offer, why don't you and I just go to the sale without their reps. That way, instead of getting 25 per cent of the royalties, we will each get 50 per cent."

My initial reaction to his proposal was one of disbelief. There was so much money involved. I was rather young at the time and relatively new in the business.

I told the man that I would get back to him. I almost ran back to the office to tell our management team what had happened. They were in shock at the depth of this deceit. One of the management team phoned the questionable land-man and told him that our company was completely against doing what he proposed. In fact, we decided to drop out of the sale altogether. I was deeply impressed by the honesty and courage of our team, which decided without hesitation to back away from this situation despite the potential loss of a lot of money.

In the above situation, we can see courage-at-cost enacted on two levels – personal and corporate:

- the young landman staying true to his principles in the face of temptation
- a whole company choosing the less lucrative but morally correct response to a clearly unethical proposal.

Courage in the workplace takes many forms: confronting a co-worker or your boss when an obvious breach of ethics occurs; speaking up at a team meeting when it is clear that your opinion differs significantly from everyone else's; making it a point not to engage in office gossip and encouraging others to avoid it as well; taking a stand against a bully; promoting an issue of social justice or care for the environment, even if this means doing so without a lot of company support; and so forth. Think about your most courageous moment at work. It is important to celebrate even small victories of courage, for they can lead to bigger ones as one success builds on another.

The Commuter Retreat (described in Chapter 1) is an op-portunity to look clearly at a challenging situation at one's place of work. Such was the case with a businessman I will call Kevin. I met Kevin through a mutual friend. At the time he made the retreat he was dealing with a conflict of interest at work. (Conflict of interest refers to a situation when someone has competing professional or personal obligations that would make it difficult to fulfill his or her duties fairly to either of the parties involved.) Kevin's boss had asked him to handle a transaction with a client whom Kevin had dealt with in the past. The circumstances were such that Kevin felt he had to turn down the assignment, but he was afraid to do so, as it might put him in an unfavourable light with his boss or even jeopardize his job. I suggested he bring his fears to God in prayer. This issue dominated the retreat as he prayed reflectively over different Gospel passages where Jesus faced his fears and helped his disciples do the same. By the time the retreat ended, Kevin found himself at peace.

With new courage, he approached his boss and explained his dilemma to her. Because he had worked through his fears and anxieties in a prayerful way, he was able to present his position in a non-threatening manner. His boss, for her part, heard what Kevin was saying and excused him from the situation. Not only were there no negative repercussions as a result of this issue, but not long after, Kevin was promoted to a new position in the company.

The ancient philosopher Cicero wrote of the courageous person as having "greatness of soul." In his classical treatise on moral goodness, *De Officiis*, he defined courage in the following way:

> All true courage and greatness of soul are best seen in two qualities.
>
> First, indifference to external conditions – which is born of the conviction that a human should esteem and desire and seek only what is seemly and honorable, that such a one should bow the knee to no master, and should yield neither to passion nor to the vicissitudes of chance. Second, eagerness, as a result of the mental attitude just described, to do things that are most vital and useful, but also that are very difficult and dangerous alike to the appurtenances of life and to life itself ... By two clear insignia this estate may be

recognized: first, the conviction that righteousness is the only good, and second, absolute self-mastery.[145]

Kevin clearly came to the fullness of Cicero's teaching.

Three other people who came to "greatness of soul" through a willingness to risk losing their jobs by bravely seeking the truth are Sherron Watkins, Cynthia Cooper, and Coleen Rowley. They were named *Time* magazine's Persons of the Year in 2002 for doing the right thing as whistle-blowers. (A whistle-blower is typically an employee who reports company, or government, criminal misconduct publicly in order to have corrective action taken.)[146] Because this kind of disclosure is not popular in a company or government agency, many organizations now have anonymous phone lines to protect employees' identities and the confidential nature of the information they wish to share.

Sherron Watkins was the Vice President for Corporate Development at Enron. In the summer of 2001, she wrote a letter to then chairman Kenneth Lay, warning him that the company's methods of accounting were improper. In January, a congressional subcommittee investigating Enron's collapse released her letter, and she reluctantly became a public figure. Coleen Rowley, an FBI staff attorney, caused a sensation with a memo to FBI Director Robert Mueller about how the bureau ignored pleas from her Midwest field office requesting that Zacarias Moussaoui (who has since been indicted as a September 11, 2001, co-conspirator) be investigated. Cynthia Cooper, Vice President of Internal Audit at World Com, exposed the illusion that was World Com when she informed its board that the company had covered up $3.8 billion in losses through phoney bookkeeping. None of these women deliberately sought the limelight; they became public figures only because their memos were made public without their consent. By standing for the truth, they put their jobs, their health, and their privacy at risk. They are true "heroines of the heart."

Aristotle taught that there are three principle elements for courage: proper fear, proper confidence, and proper value judgment.

Proper value judgment involves prudence – being careful to avoid undesired consequences. To illustrate this point, consider the following story from Edward, an executive in his mid-30s.

I am the president of a medium-sized company that sells a particular product to the Canadian oil and natural gas industry. Traditionally, our customers have mostly been contractors who buy our product, combine it with products from other companies, and sell the finished product to large oil and gas companies.

Recently, our parent company, which is located in a different city than we are, suggested we manufacture and assemble as many components as we can, and bid for jobs without going through a contractor.

This new development placed me in a dilemma. Some of the contractors we deal with have been loyal customers since our company was started 38 years ago. Loyalty is a prized possession in our industry, and I did not want to alienate the very people who have been a significant part of our history.

The first challenge of this new policy occurred when a large oil and gas firm decided to do some major renovations in one of its facilities. They hired a well-established engineering firm to organize the project. The engineering company then sent out a request for bids, what is called in the industry "RFQ," or request for quote. Before the new policy, we would be approached by a contractor for the part we distribute after he or she had won the bid. This time we decided to bid on the entire project ourselves. However, the main competitor in the bidding would be one of our most loyal, and largest contractors. Not only that, but the CEO is an old friend of mine.

Bidding on the project ourselves was not an easy decision. I consulted my main salesman who deals daily with the contractor in question. We role-played all kinds of scenarios and talked about possible outcomes. Complicating the situation is the personality of the CEO – he is a very blunt, hard-nosed person. I phoned a representative at our parent company and brainstormed with him about the situation and asked for his advice. We finally decided to go see the CEO and explain our new policy rather than go behind his back and bid on the project. Perhaps, we thought, there might be some way we could both benefit from our parent company's change of policy. My sense was "pain now, but long-term gain." But I knew in my heart that friend or not, this was going to be a very difficult encounter; I needed courage as well as my integrity to pull this off.

When my main salesman and I arrived at the contractor's office, the first thing I noticed lying on his desk was the same RFQ that we had! Pointing to it, I said to him, "We wanted to let you know, Gary, that there is a possibility we will bid on this project ourselves." I then explained to him the reason behind this change in procedure.

His immediate response was, "If you do that you will never get any more business from us!"

I said, "We would like to see some alternatives discussed, like what might be the best resolution for both of us."

He reconsidered his initial reaction and replied, "Okay, how about a joint venture?" As a result of this meeting, we decided to both put in a proposal for the contract. Whoever won would split the project, the product, and the profit 50-50 with the other, as well as the costs.

As it turned out, Gary's company won. After the contract was awarded to his company, he phoned me and said, "In the future, Edward, if a similar situation arises, please notify me like you did this time and hopefully we can do another joint venture." And so our company entered into a new way of doing business with a long-time loyal customer.

What I learned from this experience is that it is much better in the long run to be open and honest with a customer even if, in the short-term, it is painful to do so. By doing this we not only kept a good relationship with a valuable customer, but also secured an even better reputation in the industry as an ethical company that both values loyalty and lives it.

Edward's story illustrates more than one virtue. It takes *humility* to ask for advice. It takes *honesty* and *loyalty* to resist going behind the back of a long-term customer. It takes *prudence* to prepare thoroughly for a difficult action. And it takes *integrity* to keep one's principles intact in a competitive industry.

The opposite of courage is usually described as cowardice. However, imprudence is another antonym for courage. Drawing on Aristotle, André Comte-Sponville points out that courage requires moderation, as the risks we incur must be in proportion to the ends that we seek. He writes,

> Boldness, even if extreme, is therefore virtuous only if tempered with prudence: "The virtue of a free [person]," writes Spinoza, "is seen to be as great in avoiding dangers as in overcoming them ... A free [person] chooses flight with the same tenacity, or presence of mind, as he chooses a contest." ... For every [person] there are things he [or she] can and things he [or she] cannot endure....[147]

The truth of this insight into courage became abundantly clear to me one day when I was ministering in the inner city of a large California city. I had been living in the neighbourhood for a year, and knew many of the street people. One day, I was about to walk across the street in front of the local Catholic church. I heard my name yelled from the second-floor window of the building opposite. A very angry man yelled that he had a gun and was going to kill me. He even waved the gun through the window. I said to a friend from the neighbourhood who was standing next to me, "I'd better go talk to him and calm him down."

My friend said, "Are you crazy? That man is on drugs or something. He's serious about killing you. You get out of town for a few days until he calms down." I acted on her advice and drove out to the country, where I stayed for three days. By the time I got back to the parish, the man in question was no longer a threat to my safety. That woman saved me from acting imprudently, and probably saved my life.

According to Jeffrey MacDonald, writing in *The Christian Science Monitor*, some ethicists say cultivating courage promises to be an uphill battle in the 21st century.[148] This will be true, they say, whether the enemy is terrorism, threats to the environment, bullies in the workplace, or moral decay. Taking a risk for the sake of a larger purpose runs counter to the values of a society enthralled with good health, material possessions, wealth, and social status. Then there is moral relativism, which does not recognize anything as certain. Pope Benedict XVI is well known for condemning what he calls "the dictatorship of relativism," which is especially prevalent in Europe today. This philosophical approach has as its highest goal our own ego and our own desires. Moral theologian Richard Gula expands on the theme of relativism by pointing out the difference between *personal relativists*, who use the criterion of self-satisfaction to confirm what is right or wrong ("Do your own thing" is a familiar slogan of theirs) and *social relativists*, who look to what society approves of in order to know what is morally right or wrong.[149]

The relativist stance leads Rushworth Kidder, President of the Institute for Global Ethics, in Camden, Maine, to comment, "If there are no standards to stand up for, why would anybody take a moral stand?" He urges people to teach their children about courage by looking at the lives of people of courage, and to create situations that have a responsible amount of safety in which children have a chance to take courageous actions of their own.

Men draw on "Warrior" energy to face obstacles within and without in order to live a life of integrity and courage. The feminine counterpart to the male warrior is the Amazon. To explain these two archetypes, I will draw from my book *The Masculine Spirit.*[150]

The Warrior is a basic building block of masculine psychology. This character trait makes men capable of moral outrage and principled action, but not necessarily physical combat. It includes ardent passion for a just cause and may involve feats of heroism. The Warrior, in his fullness, constitutes a total way of life. It is an aggressive stance towards life that rouses, energizes, and motivates. The Amazon finds her identity and fulfillment in managing the outside world. She is clearly focused, zealous, and energetic, and is inspired by competition, efficient and organized. She is independent and self-contained. Both the Warrior and the Amazon have the capacity for great good or great harm. They both need to be aware of their weaknesses as well as their strengths, and their need for grace. When the challenges of the world to do the right thing become too difficult, an encouraging passage from the Bible that helps me is Isaiah 41:10, 13. (The "right hand" is a symbol of strength.)

> Do not fear, for I am with you, do not be afraid, for I am your God;
> I will strengthen you, I will help you,
> I will uphold you with my victorious right hand ...
> For I, the Lord your God, hold your right hand;
> it is I who say to you, "Do not fear, I will help you."

In the face of modern temptations against the virtue of courage, James Keenan, a professor of moral theology, draws on the wisdom of Thomas Aquinas. Aquinas argued that each person ought to establish a proactive agenda. In summing up Aquinas's work on the virtues, Keenan makes three points:

- First, that every human action is a moral action ... Ordinary life is the matter for moral reflection, intention, and action.
- Second, we become what we do. Anything that we intentionally do makes us become what we are doing. For example, if I was rude to someone on my way to work this morning, I am becoming a more rude person; if I stopped to help someone in need, I am growing in compassion. In the workplace, if I intend to speak up to my domineering boss, but never do, I will never attain the assertive stance that I wish I had.
- Third, if we become what we do, then we should intend ways of acting that can shape us better into being the type of people we think we should become: persons with a proactive stance towards life.[151]

Who, then, should we become? We must challenge ourselves to become people of integrity and courage, with a concern for justice and fairness. One way we can do this is by drawing inspiration from the lives of the heroes and heroines among us, in the workplace and beyond. We will consider some of these men and women in the next section.

Physical, Moral, and Civil Courage

There are many kinds of courage. I would like to highlight three: physical, moral, and civil. We show *physical courage* when we face a serious illness or disability with dignity, endure severe hardships/danger in our workplace, or face the threat of death. We show *moral courage* when we do what we know is right in the face of possible shame, scandal, loss to our reputation, or some other personal cost, "having the courage of our convictions." *Civil courage* occurs when ordinary citizens resist what they perceive as an evil or unjust or oppressive system (government and/or government policies, for example), fully aware that the consequences of their actions may lead to physical injury, prison, or even death.

Sometimes all three of these kinds of courage are present at the same time in a human situation. In order to be inspired for our own life journey, let us consider each of these forms of courage by looking at some of the people who have lived them.

Physical Courage

Physical courage includes the capacity to endure great hardship. People with serious illnesses or disabilities, especially those who carry their cross with dignity, are prime examples of this type of courage. When I am feeling sorry for myself for some ache or pain and I see someone with a far greater physical problem, my self-pity is put in its place.

Terry Fox was a young Canadian whose battle with bone cancer inspired him to run across Canada in 1980 to raise money for cancer research – despite the fact that the cancer had already claimed one of his legs. Wearing a prosthetic leg, he ran 3,339 miles over 143 days in all weather and over all types of terrain. He stopped only when he learned that the cancer had spread to his lungs. Although Terry died less than a year later, a month short of his 23rd birthday, his "Marathon of Hope" started a movement. The Terry Fox Foundation has raised over $400 million for cancer research and treatment.

Physical courage involves patient endurance. Two people whose courage in extreme circumstances has touched me deeply are my mother and a teenager from the Blackfoot Nation. My mother was diagnosed with cancer at the age of 44. I was away at college when she learned she had the disease. When I would come home for holidays, I would find her dealing with her sickness with dignity and grace. She was a deeply spiritual person who found the courage she needed from God in prayer. She spent most of the last two months of her life in the hospital. The doctors and nurses told my father that they considered her a saint because of the way she handled the pain; she never complained. She died on Easter Sunday, two years after diagnosis.

I saw her the night before she died. As always, she was more concerned about how I was doing than with her pain. She will always be a model for me in dealing with physical illness.

I met Amber Crossguns when I lived at Holy Trinity Mission on a Blackfoot Reserve (Reservation) in southern Alberta. She was a lively child of eight when I first met her family. Amber loved nature. After visits home, I used to bring her rocks and shells from California, which delighted her no end. She grew into a very accomplished teenager – a star basketball player and an artist. I have her painting of Our Lady of Guadalupe, which is quite good. She was well liked by her peers. And she was a spiritual person – reflective and prayerful. In short, her life was filled with promise. But at the age of seventeen, she came down with an illness that baffled the doctors. At the beginning of her treatment, she was misdiagnosed and given the wrong medicine, which made her condition worse. Whenever I visited her in the hospital, I was impressed with her positive attitude, her inner strength, and her tremendous courage. Here was a teenager showing us adults how to handle pain and extreme discomfort with courageous endurance. Her body finally gave out from the physical ordeal, but her spirit remained strong to the end.

In my life as a Jesuit, I have been asked at times to go into situations where there is danger and the possibility of physical harm. Once, in the early 1980s, I went to the Falls Road in Belfast, Northern Ireland, where much of the violence occurred during the time of "the Troubles." Another time I travelled to South Africa, before apartheid ended, to give talks on the social mission of the Catholic Church, which emphasizes social justice and human rights.[152] My initial response to going to these places was excitement, as I have a spirit of adventure. However, as the time approached to depart, fear set in – usually the fear of physical harm.

I used a prayer for inner freedom (described earlier in this chapter) in the face of physical danger. I would simply acknowledge my fear and then ask God for freedom from the fear of physical injury. Twice I went to South Africa. Before my second trip, now knowing the dangers full well, I was given a passage from the Bible to encourage me. So apt was this reading that I felt the presence of the Holy Spirit in the room with me:

> Listen to me, you who pursue righteousness, you who seek the Lord.
> Look to the rock from which you were hewn ...
>
> Awake, awake, put on strength, O arm of the Lord! ...
>
> I, it is I who comfort you. Can you then fear mortal man, who is human only, to be looked upon as grass,
> And forget the Lord, your maker, who stretched out the heavens
> and laid the foundations of the earth?
> All the day you are in constant dread of the fury of the oppressor;
> But when he sets himself to destroy, what is there of the oppressor's fury?
> (Isaiah 51:1, 9, 12-13, NAB)

Perhaps this is the insight that martyrs gain as they face torture and death for their beliefs. I think of Miguel Pro, a young Mexican Jesuit. Standing before a firing squad, he yelled, "*Viva Christo Rey!*" (Long live Christ the King!) as the guns went off and ended his life. I think of Archbishop Oscar Romero of El Salvador, assassinated while celebrating Mass. Before his death, he said, "If they kill me, I will be resurrected in the Salvadorian people." These brave men, and other men and women who give their lives in defence of their faith, experience the redemptive power of courage, as did Jesus on the cross.

Some occupations include physical danger as part of their job descriptions. Firefighters and men and women who work in law enforcement are obvious examples. Many of them gave their lives in the burning towers of the World Trade Center on September 11, 2001. Commercial fishermen face serious dangers on the sea in terrible weather. People working in the oil business say a particularly dangerous job in their industry is the effort to contain oil blowouts, which can occur because of the highly combustible nature of oil, pressure build-up, faulty equipment, or human error. Such occupational hazards draw on human courage, as well as mechanical help, to protect the public.

Moral Courage

For the Christian, courage is expressed in deeds of love, justice, and compassion. In the course of this book, we have learned about people who exemplify moral courage: the petroleum landman, for example, who took a stand for honesty and integrity in the workplace, and the three whistle-blowers in the corporate world and the government. I am also mindful of those who prosecute white-collar crime, for they must go up against men and women of incredible financial power;[153] of Nancy Pelosi, the first female Speaker of the House, who promoted raising the minimum wage, who sees global warming as a real threat to the entire world, and who bravely challenged then President Bush on his handling the war in Iraq; of Ralph Nader, tireless advocate of consumer rights and other social justice issues since the early 1960s; and of former Vice-President Al Gore, for his courage in exposing the myths and misconceptions regarding global warming. What do these and others like them have in common? What do *we* need to be agents of change in our own part of the world? I suggest six "movements" of moral courage:

1. The courage to *see* unethical behaviour and injustice, in the workplace and elsewhere.
2. The courage to *hear* the cries of those who are in need, who are treated unfairly or unjustly.
3. The courage to *listen* to the voice of one's conscience.

4. The courage to *choose* to go against the tide of public opinion, in the pursuit of the truth.

5. The courage to *stand alone*, if necessary, or to risk losing friends (see moral loneliness, as explained in Chapter 2) in taking a moral stand.

6. The courage of *commitment*, of staying the course for the long haul with patient endurance.

A biblical passage that speaks to these movements of moral courage is found in the Book of the prophet Isaiah, in the section of Isaiah known as the songs of the Servant.

The Lord God has given me the tongue of a teacher,
that I may know how to sustain the weary with a word.
Morning by morning he wakens – wakens my ear
to listen as those who are taught.

The Lord God has opened my ear, and I was not rebellious,
I did not turn backward ...

The Lord God helps me; therefore I have not been disgraced;
therefore I have set my face like flint,
and I know that I shall not be put to shame.
(Isaiah 50:4-5, 7)

Martin Luther King Jr. placed his vision for moral courage in his "I Have a Dream" speech at the Lincoln Memorial in Washington, DC, on August 28, 1963:

I have a dream that one day this nation will rise up and live out the true meaning of its creed: "We hold these truths to be self-evident: that all men are created equal."

I have a dream that one day on the red hills of Georgia the sons of former slaves and the sons of former slave owners will be able to sit down together at the table of brotherhood.

I have a dream that one day even the state of Mississippi, a state sweltering with the heat of injustice, sweltering with the heat of oppression, will be transformed into an oasis of freedom and justice.

I have a dream that my four little children will one day live in a nation where they will not be judged by the color of their skin but by the content of their character.

I have a dream today.[154]

Robert F. Kennedy, former United States Attorney General and champion of the rights of African-Americans, recognized how challenging it is for human beings to go against the grain. Still, he gave the following message on moral courage at the University of Capetown, South Africa, in 1966, during the time of apartheid:

Few will have the greatness to bend history; but each of us can work to change a small portion of events, and in the total of all those acts will be written the history of this generation ... it is from numberless diverse acts of courage and belief that human history is thus shaped.

Each time a person stands up for an ideal, or acts to improve the lot of others, or strikes out against injustice, he or she sends forth a tiny ripple of hope, and crossing each other from a million different centers of energy and daring, those ripples build a current which can sweep down the mightiest walls of oppression and resistance.[155]

This is true of a government, a corporation, a church, or any institution that is in need of renewal and reform. In terms of our faith, we can learn from the Bible and other sacred texts where to put our ultimate trust as we act with courage for social change. Psalm 146, for example, reminds us to put our trust in God, and not in mere mortals.

Happy [blessed] are those whose help is the God of Jacob,
whose hope is in the Lord their God,
who made heaven and earth,

the sea, and all that is in them;
who keeps faith forever.
(Psalm 146:5-6)

Civil Courage

Civil courage is also known as political courage – when civilians stand up, despite possible personal cost, against something unjust. Civil courage includes moral bravery and may include physical valour.

The Hebrew Scriptures (Old Testament) contain a notable example of political courage in the Second Book of Samuel (chapters 11 and 12). King David was one of the greatest of Israel's kings. He was a man with power and prestige. However, he had, like all of us, moral weaknesses. His most glaring weakness was his desire for the wife of a man named Uriah, a loyal soldier in the Israelite army. To make sure he could have the man's wife, David sent Uriah to the front of a battle, where the fighting was most intense. Uriah was killed. After a period of mourning had passed, David took the woman, Bathsheba, into his home as his wife.

God was displeased with what David had done, and sent the prophet Nathan to confront David. Nathan told the king a story.

> Nathan said, "There were two men in a certain city, the one rich and the other poor. The rich man had very many flocks and herds; but the poor man had nothing but one little ewe lamb, which he had bought. He brought it up, and it grew up with him and with his children; it used to eat of his meager fare, and drink from his cup, and lie in his bosom, and it was like a daughter to him. Now there came a traveler to the rich man, and he was loath to take one of his own flock or herd to prepare for the wayfarer who had come to him, but he took the poor man's lamb, and prepared that for the guest, who had come to him." [The two men are David and

Uriah; David had taken over his predecessor King Saul's harem, so he had many wives.]

David burned with anger against the man in the story and said to Nathan, "As the Lord lives, the man who has done this deserves to die; he shall restore the lamb fourfold, because he did this thing, and because he had no pity."

Then Nathan said to David, "You are the man! Thus says the Lord, the God of Israel: I anointed you king over Israel, and I rescued you from the hand of Saul; I gave you your master's house, and your master's wives into your bosom, and gave you the house of Israel and of Judah; and if that had been too little, I would have added much more. Why have you despised the word of the Lord, to do what is evil in his sight? You have struck down Uriah the Hittite with the sword and have taken his wife to be your wife and have killed him with the sword of the Ammonites...."

David said to Nathan, "I have sinned against the Lord." (2 Samuel 12:1-9, 13)

One can only imagine the depth of courage Nathan needed to confront the king.

The modern world has seen this kind of courage from men and women who have challenged injustice and corruption on both local and national scales. Three courageous people whose political actions changed others for the better are Rosa Parks, Beyers Naude, and Aung San Suu Kyi.

On December 1, 1955, Rosa Parks, tired and on her way home from a full day's work as a seamstress, refused to give up her seat to a white man in the white section of a bus in Montgomery, Alabama. She was arrested. By her simple gesture of defiance, she became the inspiration for a fourteen-month boycott that ended segregation in the city bus system. The US Congress proclaimed her the mother of the modern civil rights movement.

Beyers Naude was known during the time of apartheid in South Africa as the bravest white man in the country. The son of one of the founders of the white supremacist group Broederbond, Beyers was a Dutch Reformed minister, a leading member of the religion that supported the apartheid system. He was eventually forced out of the church because he realized that his government was built on lies. There were three steps to this reversal. First, he discovered that the biblical basis of apartheid was false, which led him to repudiate the theological grounds for it. Second, he came face to face with the injustices of the white government when he went into a gold mine and witnessed the terrible working conditions of the black miners. Third, his conversion was made complete by the 1960 Sharpeville Massacre, where police shot and killed scores of unarmed Black protestors.

I met Beyers in 1984 during my first trip to South Africa. At the time, he was under a banning order by the government because of his outspoken criticism of the apartheid system. Banning meant he could not travel more than a five-mile radius from his home for five years. He could not attend any group meetings. And, with the exception of his family, he could meet with only one person at a time in his home. On the second day after I arrived in South Africa, one of the sisters who was hosting my visit took me to his house. The Sister explained that Beyers could give me an understanding of the state of the country better than anyone in the Johannesburg area, where I was staying for the first week of a five-week visit. Indeed, I found Beyers to be a wealth of information. He impressed me as a man of deep integrity who loved his country and its potential for justice, and who courageously lived his beliefs even at the cost of his freedom of movement. When the country moved to democracy in 1994, he was the only Afrikaner in the ruling African National Congress delegation to hold talks with the former apartheid National Party.

Aung San Suu Kyi was born in Rangoon, the daughter of Burma's national hero, General Aung San, who led the struggle for independence from Britain. (The general was assassinated in 1947.) Her education spanned the globe. From 1969 to 1971, she was Assistant Secretary to the Advisory Committee on Administrative and Budgetary Questions for the United Nations in New York. She returned to Myanmar (formerly Burma) in 1988 to look after her sick mother. While she was there, student protests erupted. For some time, Burma had been under the control of a military dictatorship. As its leadership began to crumble, pro-democracy activists saw their chance to push for democratic elections. Mass uprisings were followed by a military response that killed thousands. Aung San Suu Kyi, addressing a huge crowd in Rangoon, called for a democratic government. In September 1988, the National League for Democracy (NLD) was formed, with Aung San Suu Kyi as general secretary. However, in July of the following year the military placed her under house arrest in an attempt to stop her continued participation in the democratic process. As of this writing, she is still under house arrest. In 1991, Aung San Suu Kyi was awarded the Nobel Peace Prize. The Nobel Committee wrote, "She is an extraordinary example of civil courage."[156]

These three courageous people join the likes of Mahatma Gandhi, the Dalai Lama, Nelson Mandela, Dorothy Day, Martin Luther King Jr., Helen Caldicott, and countless others who risk their lives for the welfare of their countries. Their commitment to the common good benefits all of humanity.

In this time of globalization, business leaders have the opportunity to act with political courage as well.

- Companies, on their own or in concert with others in the same industry, can join together to try to change unethical behaviour in a host country.
- Those who decide on this course of action can set timelines for visible, positive results with the understanding that they will quit the country if significant changes are not forthcoming.

- Businesses can refuse to go into a country that has a record of bribery, actions against human rights, or other unethical behaviour.

An excellent resource for companies is "The Global Sullivan Principles of Corporate Social Responsibility." Established by the late Reverend Leon Sullivan in 1999, these eight principles promote the global common good in a thorough and effective way. Sullivan described the objectives of the Principles as supporting economic, social and political justice by companies wherever they do business. Companies that endorse the principles promise to

> respect the law, and as a responsible member of society we will apply these Principles with integrity consistent with the legitimate role of business. We will develop and implement company policies, procedures, training and internal reporting structures to ensure commitment to these Principles throughout our organization. We believe the application of these Principles will achieve greater tolerance and better understanding among peoples, and advance the culture of peace.[157]

Here are the eight Principles.
Accordingly, we will:

- Express our support for universal human rights and, particularly, those of our employees, the communities within which we operate and parties with whom we do business.
- Promote equal opportunity for our employees at all levels of the company with respect to issues such as color, race, gender, age, ethnicity or religious beliefs, and operate without unacceptable worker treatment such as the exploitation of children, physical punishment, female abuse, involuntary servitude or other forms of abuse.
- Respect our employees' voluntary freedom of association.

- Compensate our employees to enable them to meet at least their basic needs and provide the opportunity to improve their skill and capability in order to raise their social and economic opportunities.
- Provide a safe and healthy workplace; protect human health and the environment; and promote sustainable development.
- Promote fair competition including respect for intellectual and other property rights, and not offer, pay or accept bribes.
- Work with governments and communities in which we do business to improve the quality of life in those communities – their educational, cultural, economic and social well-being – and seek to provide training and opportunities for workers from disadvantaged backgrounds.
- Promote the application of these Principles by those with whom we do business.

We will be transparent in our implementation of these Principles and provide information which demonstrates publicly our commitment to them.[158]

Clearly, it takes courage and commitment to live these principles. In some countries, to live them is downright subversive.

Daring to Risk

We need the virtue of courage for both the inner and outer journey. Courage helps us to face our fears and other emotional obstacles to doing the right thing regardless of possible personal cost. Implicit in this virtue is the dynamic of risk. The following poem, by an anonymous author, illustrates the many facets of risk.

To laugh is to risk appearing a fool.
To weep is to risk appearing sentimental.
To reach out to another is to risk involvement.
To expose feelings is to risk rejection.
To place your dreams before the crowd is to risk ridicule.
To love is to risk not being loved in return.
To go forward in the face of overwhelming odds is to risk failure.

But risks must be taken because the greatest hazard in life is to risk nothing.
The person who risks nothing, does nothing, has nothing, is nothing.
He may avoid suffering and sorrow, but he cannot learn, feel, change, grow, or love.
Chained to his certitudes, he is a slave.
He has forfeited his freedom.

Only a person who dares to risk is free.

You may be thinking, "but what can one person, even one company, do to make a difference in the struggle for global human rights?" I love the Dalai Lama's response to such a concern: "If you think you are too small to make a difference, try sleeping with a mosquito."

The prophet Jeremiah – no stranger to fear, to the necessity of taking a risk, or to the need for courage to fulfill the mission entrusted to him by God – has the last word on the subject of fear:

Blessed are those who trust in the Lord,
whose trust is the Lord.
They shall be like a tree planted by water,
sending out its roots by the stream.
It shall not fear when heat comes,
and its leaves shall stay green;
in the year of drought it is not anxious,
and it does not cease to bear fruit.
(Jeremiah 17:7-8)

9

Furthering the Reign of God
(Or, Building the Kingdom)

This is love, that we walk according to [God's] commandments;
this is the commandment just as you have heard it
from the beginning – you must walk in it.
—2 John 6

In the course of this book we have considered a variety of ways
we can be blessed as we engage in our work. We began with
the basis of all good decisions, the virtue of wisdom.

From there we embarked on a study of six necessary qualities
for an ethically successful career: integrity, honesty, compassion,
forgiveness, generosity, and courage. In addition, we considered
the quality of compassion as it relates to the environment. Each
of these blessings not only enhances our moral life, but also has
a salutary effect on society at large. In religious terms, we are
participating in building what the synoptic Gospels (Matthew,
Mark and Luke) call the kingdom of God.[159]

Many of us are used to thinking of the kingdom or reign
of God as referring only to the end time, to eternal life, when
God's rule will be all encompassing. Indeed, the full realization
of God's reign lives in the future. In this sense of the kingdom,
Christians of all denominations speak in eschatological terms
– eschatology being a more or less organized account of the
final age of salvation inaugurated by the incarnation of Jesus
the Christ and by his paschal mystery (Jesus' death, resurrec-

tion, and mission of the Holy Spirit). Theologian Donald Gelpi describes this understanding of the kingdom and the disposition for entry into it:

> All the synoptic gospels agree that entry into the kingdom requires a repentance which precludes all forms of religious self-righteousness.
>
> All agree that in the person and ministry of Jesus the reign of God has already arrived even though its full realization lies in the future. In the last analysis, it must await the second coming.[160]

The kingdom of God has more than one meaning, however. Here we will consider two other levels in order to see how what we do in the present does or does not participate in furthering the goals of the kingdom and in serving the kingdom now. To aid in this endeavour, we must realize that we are in the "already/not-yet" dimension of salvation history. The saving event has occurred in the birth, life, death, and resurrection of Jesus, but it is not complete; it has not been universally extended. So we are living in the interim: the interval between the dawning of the new order of life and its victory.[161]

In his perceptive book *Go and Do Likewise*, Bill Spohn leads us from the first level of meaning of the kingdom of God to the second. He does this by asking the following questions: Is the *basileia tou theou* (God's reign or realm) a place, a "kingdom," or is it a region of authority, a "reign"? Is it a state of mind and heart or a social reality? Is it an event that is breaking into history or is it the goal of history?[162] In other words, does it have geographical boundaries, or is it more spiritual and moral in nature?

When Jesus spoke of the kingdom, he was speaking to a people who were hoping for a great leader to rid them of Roman occupation. They were interested in a temporal kingdom, a nation free from outside constraints. Jesus spent much of his teaching time dispelling this idea. Theologian Elizabeth Johnson points out that the kingdom signifies the state of affairs that will exist when human beings fully acknowledge that God is the One in whom their ultimate identity rests.[163] This is true wisdom. When we pray the Our Father, the prayer that Jesus taught us – especially the words "Thy kingdom come; thy will be done on earth as it is in heaven" – we are asking that we may have the courage to do what God wants of us in both our personal and our professional lives.

Scripture scholars agree that the kingdom or reign of God was at the heart of Jesus' ministry. In describing the kingdom, he often used parables.

Parable means comparison. Parables subvert accepted understandings in order to open the listener or reader to a new view of things. They begin by describing a familiar world, but then introduce a startling development that calls the reality of that world into question. In Jesus' case, the comparison helps the listener understand what the Kingdom is. By the use of this story form, Jesus was able to express some of the transcendent reality of God and God's values through common, everyday objects and activities.

For example, in the Gospel according to Matthew, Jesus told a large crowd at the Lake of Galilea eight parables about the kingdom (sometimes he used the term "kingdom of heaven" instead of "kingdom of God"):

- the sower
- the weeds among the wheat
- the mustard seed
- the yeast
- the treasure buried in a field
- the merchant searching for fine pearls
- the net thrown into the sea that collects fish of every kind, and
- the head of a household who brings from his storeroom both the new and the old.

(Matthew 13:1-53)

When his disciples asked why he spoke in parables, Jesus told them it was his way of announcing what had been hidden from the foundation of the world (Matthew 13:35).

Jesus inaugurated the kingdom of God. When the Pharisees asked him when the kingdom would come, he replied, "In fact, the kingdom of God is among you" (Luke 17:21). Through his preaching and healing ministry, the kingdom began to arrive in people's lives. Consider what he accomplished:

- he restored some people to physical health, allowing them to return as full members of their community: they had been ostracized because of their infirmities;
- he raised people from the dead, including Lazarus (John 11:1-44) and the only son of a widow (Luke 7:11-17);
- he forgave people their sins;
- he exorcised demons, overthrowing the power of evil (Luke 11:20);
- he brought joy back to people's hearts, such as through healings and through the wedding feast of Cana (John 2:1-11).

Jesus' understanding of the kingdom involves an intimate friendship with God that is inclusive of our neighbour. One of the scribes asked him, "Which commandment is the first of all?" Jesus answered,

> "The Lord our God, the Lord is one; you shall love the Lord your God with all your heart, and with all your soul, and with all your mind, and with all your strength. The second is this, You shall love your neighbour as yourself. There is no other commandment greater than these." (Mark 12:28-34)

It is in loving our neighbour that we come to the third level of meaning of the kingdom of God.

The Parable of the Good Samaritan, which we explored in in the chapters on integrity, compassion, and generosity, shows us the kind of concern God wants us to have for those in need.

Bill Spohn, pointing out that the kingdom continues to enter into history through human response, writes, "God does not reign over us unless we agree to let it happen."[164] God needs our co-operation. Don Gelpi indicates that this level of understanding the Kingdom involves faithful service to the Lord. We are to live in a state of preparation for the coming of the Son of God: "Readiness means the practical living of the gospel."[165]

In terms of the workplace, being in the kingdom means staying true to our faith values with courage and commitment regardless of how difficult that might be at times. Being in the kingdom means minimizing "non-kingdom moments"[166] by living lives of integrity. Certainly there are challenges to living an ethical life. We have considered some of these in this book:

- properly using our inner freedom to create and maintain just corporate systems and structures;
- writing and upholding codes of conduct;
- offering all the employees in an organization a just wage and benefits;
- challenging the large discrepancies between executive compensation and employees' salaries; and
- taking practical steps to safeguard the environment.

We have also read about men and women who, by their ethical actions, are staying true to their basic faith values. I learned a lot about moral values from my parents and teachers. From my mother, I learned how to be compassionate to those in financial need. She had a heart as big as the city we lived in. From my father, who worked hard to support the family, I learned the values of responsibility and hard work. Two other significant adults, through their spirituality and commitment to ethics in the workplace, were kingdom people for me and for all who met them: Bob Smith and Rube Hayden.

Bob was a car salesman who eventually owned his own dealership. In Los Angeles, where he lived and worked, he had a reputation for being a man of honour, honesty, and great generosity. He and his wife, Celeste, were friends of my parents before I was born, so I had the benefit of his example from childhood. Though we were not related by blood, Bob was like an uncle to me. By the time I reached my teens, Bob was well established in the auto industry, but he was not one to boast about it; there was a humility in him that was refreshing.

Rube Hayden, like my father, was in the food business; that was where they met. He and his wife, Virginia, and their family became good friends of ours. This Kentucky gentleman had moved to Los Angeles as a young man. He started out simply, but became very successful in business. He was also a gracious and kind person.

Bob and Celeste, like Rube and Virginia, were deeply religious people. What impressed me as a teenager about Bob and Rube was that there never seemed to be a disconnect between their faith life, their home life, and their work life. Both Bob and Rube sustained their core values in highly competitive industries. I am sure they had their challenging moral moments at work. Everyone does.

Each of the major world religions has a vision of living in a way that furthers the reign of God. After all, as we saw in Chapter 1, all of them have a version of the Golden Rule. When we live this rule in our personal and professional lives, we are living in the kingdom. Other directives help to guide people of faith in their moral actions as well. Here are some examples from Judaism, Christianity, and Islam.

In the Hebrew Scriptures (Old Testament), God gives the Israelite people the Ten Commandments (Exodus 20:1-17) to guide their moral path. Through the prophets, God urges the people to live lives of love and service, of justice and compassion.

Jesus gives us an extension of the Ten Commandments in the eight Beatitudes (Matthew 5:1-12). We are to be poor in spirit, that is, free of inordinate attachments to material possessions, and trust in the Father; to mourn our own and others' losses; to walk humbly and not consider ourselves superior to others, no matter how much earthly power we have; to crave justice for all, with a special concern for the least powerful of our brothers and sisters; to love even our enemies and pray for those who persecute us; to stand fast to our core faith values; to seek peace and reconciliation above all things; and go to God for help when our cross seems too difficult to bear.

Islam has five primary obligations, called "The Five Pillars." They are *Shahadah*, or profession of faith in God; *Salah*, the belief that individuals have a direct relationship with God; *Zakat*, or almsgiving for the benefit of the poor and the needy; *Sawim*, fasting during the holy month of Ramadan as a form of personal worship in which a believer's sensitivity is heightened to the sufferings of the poor; and *Hajj*, the pilgrimage to Mecca to participate in the most significant spiritual gathering of Muslims from all over the world.[167]

As we have seen, the kingdom or reign of God has three levels of meaning:

1. The end-time or eternal life when God's rule will be all-encompassing.
2. Jesus' inauguration of the kingdom and his ways of proclaiming it.
3. Our role in furthering the goals of the kingdom in the here and now by our faith and virtuous conduct.

Our role in building the kingdom is essential. An honest appraisal of our strengths and weaknesses, our gifts and talents, helps us to make wise decisions that help further the goals of the kingdom. Two role models who can assist us in this discernment are Marianne Williamson, founder of the Peace Alliance and Project Angel Food, and Rabbi Abraham Joshua Heschel, who was a well-respected Jewish theologian and champion of civil rights in the United States.

Williamson writes,

Our deepest fear is not that we are inadequate. Our deepest fear is that we are powerful beyond measure. It is our light, not our darkness, that frightens us most. We ask ourselves, who am I to be brilliant, gorgeous, talented and fabulous? Actually, who are you not to be? You are a child of God! Your playing small doesn't serve the world. There is nothing enlightened about shrinking so that other people won't feel insecure around you. We were born to manifest the glory of God within us. It is not just in some of us; it's in everyone. And, as we let our light shine, we unconsciously give other people permission to do the same. As we are liberated from our own fear, our presence automatically liberates others.[168]

In his book *I Asked for Wonder*, Rabbi Heschel wrote,

Looking at myself from the perspective of society, I am an average person.

Facing myself intimately, immediately, I regard myself as unique, as exceedingly precious, not to be exchanged for anything else.

No one will live my life for me, no one will think my thoughts for me or dream my dreams.

In the eyes of the world, I am an average man. But to my heart I am not an average man.

To my heart I am of great moment.

The challenge I face is how to actualize the quiet eminence of my being.[169]

We can safely say that the love of God flourishes in the kingdom. It is a realm of salvation, not judgment. The kingdom thrives where freedom overcomes fear to act ethically in all circumstances. And the kingdom is inclusive in its outreach – participants can be poor or rich, successful or failures in the world's eyes, from every race and culture, from one end of the world to the other. Theologian Elizabeth Johnson sums it up well:

> The reign of God is the situation that results when God's will is really done. What is God's will? As revealed in Jesus, God's will is our well-being. God wants the wholeness, the healing, and the salvation of every creature and of all of us taken together. The reign of God, then, involves justice and peace among everyone, healing and wholeness everywhere, fullness of life enjoyed by all.[170]

Let us continue to build it together.

Appendix A

Centering Prayer

In the centre of our being, God lives. Centering prayer is one method of praying that enables us to experience the presence of God. This simple method of entering into contemplative prayer is also a powerful tool for transforming our life.[171] Here are five steps to engage in this form of prayer:

1. To ensure that your prayer has a social as well as a personal dimension, make a simple request to God that this time of prayer will be offered for someone or for some situation in the world that needs God's special grace. For example, peace in a war-torn country, deeper compassion for the earth, for the homeless, for refugees, and so forth.

2. Find a quiet place. Simply sit, relaxed, enjoying your own inner calm and the silence. For a couple of minutes, be attentive to the quiet, knowing that you are in the presence of God who loves you. ("Be still and know that I am God." – Psalm 46:10)

3. After a time, perhaps a single word or short phrase will arise in your consciousness, one that captures your receptive response to God's inner presence. Or choose a simple word that the mind can easily retain – for example, "Jesus," "Lord," "Spirit," "Love," or a phrase such as "Jesus have mercy" or "Lord Jesus Christ have mercy on me." It is helpful if you say this word or phrase in rhythm with

your breathing. The word or phrase you use is sometimes called a *mantra* (from the Sanskrit *man* — to think, *tra* — to liberate). As *The Cloud of Unknowing*, a spiritual book written in the fourteenth century by an anonymous author, says, "Let this little word [or short phrase] represent to you God in all of God's fullness and nothing less than the fullness of God. Let nothing except God sway in your mind and heart."

4. After a while, you may find that you do not need the word or phrase; if this happens, just rest in the quiet. Centre all your attention and desire on God, leaving your faculties at peace, allowing God to draw you into a perfect prayer of adoration, love, and praise. Let it happen; don't force it. Whenever you find yourself distracted by a thought or image, simply return to your word or phrase to recentre yourself.

5. Spend between 20 and 30 minutes in prayer. When this time is up, move slowly to silent awareness. Next, make a conscious interior prayer of thanksgiving, such as the Lord's Prayer, for this time of contemplation, Say each word slowly, savouring its meaning.

Appendix B

Meditating on the Gospels

God speaks to us first: This is the fundamental truth that makes it possible for us to pray to God in the first place. God desires to communicate with us.

God invites us to listen: Our response to God's initial move is to listen to what God is saying. Listening is the basic attitude of prayer.

- *How to go about listening*: Jesus often went somewhere alone to pray to his Father. Find a quiet place, indoors or outdoors. We live in a time of many cares and commitments, much noise and excitement. We should not feel we must blot out all these distractions, for such anxiety could get between us and the Creator. The Word became flesh; the Risen Lord can speak to us even in the midst of the noise and confusion of everyday life. Try listening to the sounds around you in an attentive manner to quiet your mind.

- *Choose a passage from one of the Gospels*: Pick a passage where Jesus is engaged in some activity. Read the passage slowly and meditatively. Do not be in a hurry to cover all the material. Try to immerse yourself in the scene. Put yourself in the place of the persons involved with Jesus: for example, a blind man desiring sight (Mark 10:46-52); parents seeking a blessing for their children (Luke 18:15-17); or the disciples with Jesus at the Last Supper (John 13:1-20). Try to take the attitude Jesus calls for in the passage. Know that the people Jesus met in his earthly life were very much like us. They had their own fears, concerns, difficulties, talents, and gifts. If you are reading a passage where every word seems to carry special meaning for you, it is time to *pause*. Savour each word, turning it over in your mind and heart. You will know it is time to pause when

- you feel a new way of being with Jesus or you know him in a new way
- you are moved to a deeper realization of God's love for you
- you find yourself able to love others more completely
- you feel lifted up in spirit
- you are moved to do something good
- you are at peace
- you are just happy and content to be in God's presence.

This is God speaking directly to you in the words of Scripture. Do not hurry on. Wait until you are no longer moved by the experience.

Don't be discouraged if nothing seems to be happening during your time of prayer, or if you encounter distractions. God is still present, even if you do not feel his presence. Ask for patience. You may wish to speak to God about the things you are interested in, the things you want to thank him for, your joys, your sorrows, your hopes, your aspirations.

- *End the time of prayer with the Lord's Prayer.*[172]

Appendix C

Prayer Using Your Imagination
(Application of the Senses)

S *tep 1*: Find a place where you are alone and uninhibited in your response to God's presence. If you pray at home, you may have to exercise some creativity here, depending on the amount of activity where you live. A father of six told me that when his children were little, he would pray in the bathtub! His wife would mind the children during his prayer time. (Fortunately, they had more than one bathroom.) A woman, also with children at home, related to me that she prays in the car in the garage while her husband looks after their children. Some people find a special place in their home or garden, a sacred setting that offers the solitude they need.

Step 2: Choose a Gospel story from Jesus' life. Read the passage through once in order to familiarize yourself with the scene and the people. Imagine the place and the persons in the story. Use your five senses to explore the setting of the passage. Is it in the city or the countryside? Is it hot? Daytime or nighttime? Friendly or threatening? (Your senses are not an end in themselves, simply a method to help you enter into the story.) Start as a spectator. Next, be in the scene as one of the characters or as yourself.

Step 3: Focus on the person of Jesus. What does he look like? Notice what he is wearing. What is he doing? What is he saying?

Step 4: Reflect on yourself. Does the passage speak to you about your own life – for example, your need for healing, for greater courage, for deeper compassion, for the grace to forgive someone who has offended you?

If, during the course of the meditation, your mind becomes distracted, bring yourself back to prayer by rereading the story. You may have to only read a few words to re-enter the scene.

Step 5: Rest in the presence of God for as long as you are able.

Step 6: To end this time of prayer, thank God – Father, Son, or Holy Spirit – in some way.

Appendix D

The Freedom Prayer

The Freedom Prayer can be used to address excessive emotional needs as well as fears that threaten to paralyze us. Both dynamics can derail our best intentions to live ethical and moral lives. Here are the steps to implement this prayer.[173]

Step 1: I become aware of a lack of freedom or of a fear, something that is upsetting my peace of mind and spirit. I find myself acting or feeling compelled to act from my false self (the negative aspects of my personality).

Step 2: I realize I cannot become free of this aspect of my persona through my own efforts; I acknowledge that only God can free me.

Step 3: I believe that God wants to free me, wants me to be more like Jesus in word and action, more my true self, because God loves me.

Step 4: I ask God for light to know what it is that I need that I am not receiving (or where I lack inner freedom). I try to name it. (Naming it is important: it heightens my self-knowledge and humility, two important features of this kind of prayer.)

Step 5: I ask God for freedom from the excessive emotional need I have named: for example, the need for approval or the need to please others, or for freedom from a debilitating fear. I pray the phrase "Lord, please free me from [name the excessive need or fear]," or words to that effect, every time I find myself acting from the unfreedom or the fear, or when I realize later that I have done so.

Step 6: I leave the healing in God's hands, like a child, with complete trust that the freedom I have asked for will be given to me. I go about my life, leaving God to take care of the healing. Therefore, it is not necessary to repeat the prayer often during the day. I say it only at the time I discover I am acting from the unfreedom or the fear. I can use this prayer at home, at work, or in any situation.

Step 7: What will be healed is the unfreedom – the excessive need, for example, not the lack of a thing, such as approval. Thus, I will be at peace whether, in this case, the need for approval is met or not. This is a great gift, especially when my integrity is at stake in a challenging ethical situation.

Step 8: Sometimes the freedom prayed for will come right away; at other times it will take a while. Sometimes God will use the opportunity to free me from more than I originally asked for: for example, from another aspect of my false self that is connected with the excessive need or fear that led to the prayer in the first place.

Step 9: It is important not to doubt (or hedge one's bets). If I am of two minds about what I am asking for, I can expect nothing to happen. Consider Jesus' words from Mark's Gospel:

> Have faith in God. I assure you that whoever tells this hill to get up and throw itself in the sea and does not doubt in his heart, but believes that what he says will happen, it will be done for him. For this reason I tell you: When you pray and ask for something, believe that you have received it, and you will be given whatever you ask for. (11:22-24).

The "hill" in this quote could be seen symbolically as the excessive emotional need or paralyzing fear from which I wish to be freed.

Notes

Introduction

1   Those who are quoted with their real names have given me permission to do so. For those who preferred anonymity, I have used fictitious names.

2   Max Oliva, S.J., *Praying the Beatitudes: A Retreat on the Sermon on the Mount* (Dublin, Ireland: Veritas Publications, 1990, reprinted 1994 and 2005).

3   John L. McKenzie, S.J., *Dictionary of the Bible* (New York: Macmillan Publishing Company, 1965), 84.

Chapter 1

4   I am drawing on two primary resources for this overview: McKenzie, *Dictionary of the Bible*, 929–35, and the *New Catholic Encyclopedia*, Volume XIV (New York: McGraw-Hill, 1967) 967–74.

5   Tom Morris, *If Aristotle Ran General Motors* (New York: Henry Holt and Company, 1997), 10.

6   McKenzie, *Dictionary of the Bible*, 931.

7   I used a variety of sources for this list: John C. Maxwell, *There's No Such Thing As "Business" Ethics* (Published by Warner Books, 2003), 22–23 (in the footnotes to the chapter he suggests two websites: www.thegoldenrule.net and www.teachingvalues.com); "The Golden Rule Across the World's Religions," a 22" x 29" colour poster designed by Scarboro Missions, which can be ordered from: Broughton's, 2105 Danforth Ave., Toronto, Ontario, Canada M4C 1K1; and Cameron Fleet, *Native American Wisdom* (Saraband Inc. P.O. Box 0032, Rowayton, CT 06853-0032).

8   http://query.nytimes.com/gst/fullpage.html?res=9807E3D61439F935A15750 C0A960958260 (accessed February 11, 2009).

9   I heard this story while attending Rabbi Michael Klein-Katz's course entitled "An Introduction to the Role of Scripture in Jewish Life and Thought" in Jerusalem in 1993.

10 David Fleming, S.J., *The Spiritual Exercises of St. Ignatius: A Literal Translation and a Contemporary Reading* (St. Louis, MO: The Institute of Jesuit Resources, 1978).

11 Fleming, *The Spiritual Exercises of St. Ignatius*, 23.

12 Fleming, *The Spiritual Exercises of St. Ignatius*, 23. (emphasis mine)

13 Warren Harbeck, "Coffee with Warren," *The Cochrane Eagle*, Alberta, Canada, December 1, 2004.

14 Donna Schaper, *Celebrate Labor Day* (Liguori, MO: Liguori Publications).

15 Walter Burghardt, S.J., "Jesus, the Wisdom of God," *The Living Pulpit* (July–September 2000), 4.

16 Anonymous

17 David Whyte, *The Heart Aroused* (New York: Currency Doubleday, 1994), v.

18 Stephen J. Patterson, "Preaching the Anti-Wisdom of Jesus," *The Living Pulpit* (July–September 2000), 11.

19 Patterson, "Preaching the Anti-Wisdom of Jesus," 10–11.

20 See "Surprised by the Gospel: Preaching as Anti-Wisdom, " by Judith Hoch Wray, *The Living Pulpit* (July–September 2000), 42–43.

21 David Irvine is the author of three books. For information on his writing and other activities, go to his website: www.david@davidirvine.com.

22 *Summa Contra Gentiles*, I, c.2, by Thomas Aquinas.

Chapter 2

23 Warren Bennis, *On Becoming a Leader* (Reading, MA: Addison-Wesley, 1994), 41, 160.

24 Confucius, *Analects*.

25 Stephen R. Covey, *The 7 Habits of Highly Effective People* (New York: Simon & Schuster, 1990), 92.

26 Suzanne Noffke, O.P., "Integrity Learned in Contemplation: Insights from Catherine of Siena," *Religious Life Review*, Vol. 42, March/April 2003. This Journal is published in Dublin, Ireland.

27 For information on Michael Josephson and his work in ethics, see www.josephsoninstitute.org.

28 John Wooden with Steve Jamison, *Wooden: A Lifetime of Observations and Reflections on and off the Court* (Chicago: Contemporary Books, 1997), 10.

29 Stephen L. Carter, *Integrity* (New York: Harper Perennial, 1996), 7. Some additional books that treat the virtue of integrity are David Irvine, *Becoming Real: Journey to Authenticity* (Sanford, FL: DC Press, 2003); Thomas G. Plante, *Do the Right Thing: Living Ethically in an Unethical World* (Oakland, CA: New Harbinger Publications, 2004, distributed in Canada by Raincoast Books); Jeffrey L. Seglin, *The Right Thing: Conscience, Profit and Personal Responsibility in Today's Business* (Rollinsford, NH: Spiro Press, 2002/2003. Each chapter is from the author's column on business ethics in *The New York Times*.)

30 David Lonsdale, *Listening to the Music of the Spirit: The Art of Discernment* (Notre Dame, IN: Ave Maria Press, 1993), 51. This is an excellent introductory book on what is known as spiritual discernment. A very good follow-up book is Thomas Green, S.J., *Weeds Among the Wheat – Discernment: Where Prayer and Action Meet* (Notre Dame, IN: Ave Maria Press, 1984).

31 Carter, *Integrity*, 26–27.

32 Leonard O. Rodrigues, MAAA, MRAIC, AIA, *Elevation West*, the magazine of the Alberta, Saskatchewan and Manitoba Association of Architects (Fall 2002 issue), 8, 10.

33 Robert C. Solomon, *A Better Way to Think About Business: How Personal Integrity Leads to Corporate Success* (New York: Oxford University Press, 2003).

34 Carter, *Integrity*, 11.

35 Fr. Ron Rolheiser, O.M.I., writes a weekly column on spirituality. This quote is from his October 20, 2002, column (see also November 16, 2003 and February 20, 2005). The column is available at www.ronrolheiser.com

36 Jean-Pierre De Caussade, S.J., *The Joy of Full Surrender* (Orleans, MA: Paraclete Press, 1986), 157.

Chapter 3

37 For a thorough biblical treatment of sin, see McKenzie, *Dictionary of the Bible*, 817–21; James F. Keenan, S.J., *Moral Wisdom*, chapter 3 (New York: Sheed and Ward, 2004), 47–65; and Richard M. Gula, S.S., *Reason Informed by Faith: Foundations of Catholic Morality* (Paulist Press: Mahwah, NJ, 1989), 89–122.

See also an online monthly newsletter I write called "Spirituality and Ethics," especially the February and March 2008 issues. These are part of a seven-part series on The Lord's Prayer. To access the newsletter, go to www.jesuits.ca. Click on News. Then click on Spirituality and Ethics (in the box on the right side of the News page).

38   Cynthia Heald, *Becoming a Woman of Excellence* (Colorado Springs, CO: NavPress, 1986), 92.

39   Carol Gilligan, *In a Different Voice: Psychological Theory and Women's Development* (Harvard University Press, 1982).

40   Robert C. Solomon and Kristine Hanson, *It's Good Business* (New York: Atheneum, 1985), 26.

41   Gula, *Reason Informed by Faith*, 7–8, 30.

42   Sheldon Alberts, "Chrétien Defies Catholic Criticism," *Calgary Herald*, August 13, 2003.

43   Morris, *If Aristotle Ran General Motors*, 120.

44   James C. Hunter, *The Servant: A Simple Story About the True Essence of Leadership* (Roseville, CA: Prima Publishing, 1998), 182. The reference to Huston Smith is on page 180. Another excellent resource is John Dalla Costa, *The Ethical Imperative: Why Moral Leadership Is Good Business* (Toronto: Harper Collins, 1998). Especially see chapter 2: "Lies."

45   http://www.quotes.net/quote/544 (accessed February 11, 2009).

Chapter 4

46   *The Spiritual Espousals and Other Works*, James A. Wiseman, OSB, trans. (Mahwah, NJ: Paulist Press, 1985), 60.

47   Donald P. McNeill, Douglas A. Morrison, and Henri Nouwen, *Compassion: A Reflection on the Christian Life* (New York: Image Books, 1983), 4.

48   Geoffrey Colvin, "The *Other* Victims of Bernie Ebbers's Fraud," *Fortune* magazine (August 8, 2005), 32.

49   See also the Book of Sirach (Ecclesiasticus) 4:1-8, for a challenging passage on showing compassion to those who are economically poor.

50   McNeill, Morrison, and Nouwen, *Compassion*, 18.

51   Jean Vanier, "At the Heart of Compassion," a booklet published by Irish Messenger Publications, 37 Lower Leeson Street, Dublin 2, Ireland. Jean Vanier, a Canadian, is the founder of L'Arche, a movement that seeks to give people who have developmental disabilities a life of dignity.

52   For a description of a third conversion experience, one that involved my living and ministering among Mexican people, please see my book *Praying the Beatitudes: A Retreat on the Sermon on the Mount* (Dublin, Ireland: Veritas Publications, 1990), 53–55.

53   Don Clark, *Loving Someone Gay* (New York: New American Library, 1977). See also James L. Empereur, S.J., *Spiritual Direction and the Gay Person* (New York: Continuum). This is a first-class resource and guidebook for both spiritual directors and homosexual persons interested in the spiritual journey.

54   Megan Boutillier, *No Is a Complete Sentence* (New York: Ballantine Books, 1995).

55   Lao Tzu, 86.

56   For signs of burnout, see J. Murray Elwood, *Not for Sale: Saving Your Soul and Your Sanity at Work* (Notre Dame, IN: Sorin Books, 2000), 35–36:
      PHYSICAL SIGNS: low energy, chronic fatigue; you wake up dreading the prospect of going to work or you come home too exhausted to eat dinner.
      EMOTIONAL SIGNS: helplessness, hopelessness, and a sense of being "trapped"; you feel that no matter how hard you work, you can't rest and you can't sit still.
      SPIRITUAL SIGNS: a loss of a sense of meaning and a sense of futility over your vocational or professional path; questions like "What's it all worth?" and "Why am I doing this?" often surface, coupled with negative feelings towards work and withdrawal from personal relationships.

57   Fr. Eamon Tobin, *How to Forgive Yourself and Others: Steps to Reconciliation* (Liguori, MO: Liguori Publications, 1993), 44.

58   Tobin, *How to Forgive Yourself and Others*, 44.

59   Dorothy Hulburt is a wife and mother. She currently serves as Director of Adult Education and Family Ministry at St. Therese Parish in San Diego, California, and has worked for over 29 years in pastoral, catechetical, and liturgical ministries. Used with permission.

60   "Our Mission, Our Values, Our Project": September 2005 (20 425 Clark-Graham Street, Baie d'Urfé, Montréal, Quebec). See also Dr. Robert Ouimet, "Spirituality in Management Reconciles Human Well-Being, Productivity, and Profits." (This resource is known as The Golden Book and is available in English, French, and Spanish from Holding O.C.B., Inc. 300 Leo-Pariseau #2120, Montréal, Québec, H2X 4B3; you can also e-mail jrouimet-ocb@qc.aira.com).

61   William C. Spohn, *Go and Do Likewise: Jesus and Ethics* (New York: Continuum, 1999), 87–91.

62   The Tomasso Corporation is connected to Dr. Robert Ouimet (see note 60).

63   William H. Taylor, Ph.D. (of the Centre for Creative Negotiating), "Creative Negotiating"; and "Negotiations and Ethics," from the Canadian Association of Petroleum Landmen's Professionalism Manual, June 1999.

64   www.christushealth.org.

65   For information on the Institute of Business Ethics (IBE), go to www.ibe.org.uk.

66   www.encana.com.

67   John D. Beckett, *Loving Monday: Succeeding in Business Without Selling Your Soul* (Downers Grove, IL: InterVarsity Press, 2001), 110.

68   *Blessed Mother Teresa* (London, UK: St. Paul's Publishing, 2003).

Chapter 5

69   *The Globe and Mail*, December 17, 2004, page E1.

70   *Under Currents*, April 18, 2005; from Downey Youell Associates of Dublin, Ireland.

71   Satish Kumar, "A Declaration of Dependence," *Spiritearth* (November 2005, Volume 16, Number 1), 2.

72   The European Foundation for the Improvement of Living and Working Conditions, an Agency of the European Commission.

73   "Is There a Green Movement in the Air?" *Fortune* magazine, Special Advertising Feature (December 12, 2005).

74 "The Writings of St. Francis of Assisi," a publication of the Franciscan Archive (see www.franciscan-archive.org).

75 *The Pope Speaks*, Vol. 35, No. 3 (May/June, 1990), 206.

76 Pierre Teilhard de Chardin, *The Future of Man* (Harper and Row, New York, 1964), 107ff. See also his *The Phenomenon of Man* (Harper & Row, 1965; new English translation title: *The Human Phenomenon*), which offers an overall synthesis of his thinking.

77 Sean McDonagh, *To Care for the Earth: A Call to a New Theology* (Santa Fe, NM: Bear and Company, 1987), 79. Note also Thomas Berry's book, *The Dream of the Earth* (San Francisco: Sierra Club Books, 1988).

78 Pierre Teilhard de Chardin, *Hymn of the Universe* (New York: Harper and Row, 1965), 68–71. Of additional interest is Teilhard's masterpiece, *The Divine Milieu* (Harper Torchbooks, 1960).

79 "Environmental Activist Models for the 1990's," by Al Fritsch, S.J., (Winter, 1989), 18–23. For information on Fr. Fritsch's work, visit www.earthhealing.info, an online collection of earth affirming writings and eco-spirituality topics.

80 http://www.petro-canada.ca/pdfs/Code_of_Business_Conduct__E.pdf, p. 14 (accessed February 11, 2009).

81 "Will Calgary Ever Be Green?" *Calgary Inc.* (April 2006), 23.

82 Vinson Brown, *Voices of Earth and Sky: The Vision Life of the Native Americans* (Happy Camp, CA: Naturegraph Publishers, Inc., 1976), 13.

83 Jane Blewett, "Impoverished People-Impoverished Earth," *Spiritearth* (November 2005), 4–5.

84 Elaine Siemsen, "Who is the Cosmic Christ?" *The Lutheran* (April 1, 2004). This is a consumer publication providing coverage and analysis of religion and philosophy.

85 Ram Dass and Paul Gorman, *How Can I Help* (New York: Alfred A. Knopf, 1985), 20.

86 Thomas Berry, *The Great Work: Our Way into the Future* (New York: Bell Tower Press, 1999). I drew from a review of the book by Bob Worcester, from the journal *Gatherings: Seeking Ecopsychology* (Summer Issue, August 2000).

87 Worcester, *Gatherings* (Summer Issue, August 2000).

88 John Pratt, "A Man with a Mission," *Nature Canada Magazine* (Spring 2002), 36.

89 Pratt, "A Man with a Mission," 37.

90 Pratt, "A Man with a Mission," 37.

91 McDonagh, *To Care for the Earth*, 131.

92 Andrew Nikiforuk, "Coal-Bed Methane: Going, Going… Gone," *Canadian Business* (September 13-26, 2004), 9–10.

93 Berry, *The Dream of the Earth*, 60.

94 Berry, *The Dream of the Earth*, 115.

95 Linda Lear, *Rachel Carson: Witness for Nature* (New York: Henry Holt Publishers, 1998).

96 http://www.catholicworker.org/dorothyday (accessed February 11, 2009).

97 http://www.albertaviews.ab.ca/aboutus.html (accessed February 11, 2009).

98 "God's Grandeur," in *Gerard Manley Hopkins: The Major Works*, edited by Catherine Phillips (Oxford University Press, 2002), 128.

99 Edward Matchett, from Painton Cowen's *Rose Windows: Art and Imagination* (London: Thames and Hudson, 1979).

Chapter 6

100 Lewis Smedes, *Forgive and Forget: Healing the Hurts We Don't Deserve* (New York: Simon & Schuster, 1984), 18.

101 Smedes, *Forgive and Forget*, 59–61.

102 Yevgeny Yevtushenko, "When One Person Reaches out with Love," from *A Precious Autobiography*, by the same author (Penguin Books, 1991).

103 I am indebted to the wisdom of Fr. Jim Hanley, S.J., retreat director and spiritual companion, for enlightening me on these eight points. For a further explanation of Point 8, see my book *The Masculine Spirit: Resources for Reflective Living*, chapter 6, "Dealing with Father Wounds" (Notre Dame, IN: Ave Maria Press, 1997). Chapter 6 explains the healing process I went through a year after my father died. The healing process eventually led to my forgiving him for some emotional wounds I received from him as a child and teenager.

104 One such organization is the International Forgiveness Institute, in Madison, Wisconsin. Go to http://www.forgiveness-institute.org for information and for a list of their publications, including back issues of their periodical, *The World of Forgiveness*.

105 Tanya Glaser, "Article Summary of Truth and Reconciliation Commission, South Africa." In *Beyond Intractability* (Conflict Research [Information] Consortium, University of Colorado, Boulder, Colorado).

106 Michael Hurley, S.J., "Reconciliation and Forgiveness," *The Jurist* (Vol. 56, No. 1, 1996), 465ff.

107 Phil Fontaine, "Ottawa Changes Framework for Residential School Compensation Claims," *Catholic New Times*, January 4, 2004.

108 The Hon. Chuck Strahl, "Date Set for Indian Residential School Apology," Indian Northern Affairs Canada, May 15, 2008. 2-3036. www.ainc-inac.gc.ca.

109 Robert J. Spitzer, S.J., *The Spirit of Leadership* (Provo, UT: Executive Excellence Publishing, 2000), 227–28.

110 Frederick Buechner, "Buechner on Forgiveness," *The Living Pulpit* (April–June 1994), 25.

111 Smedes, *Forgive and Forget*, 12.

112 Henri J. M. Nouwen, "Forgiveness: The Name of Love in a Wounded World," *Weavings* (March/April, 1992), 14.

113 Pope John Paul II, "No Peace Without Justice, No Justice Without Forgiveness," nos. 8, 10.

Chapter 7

114 Robert C. Roberts, "Just a Little Bit More: Greed and the Malling of Our Souls," *Christianity Today*, April 8, 1996, 29–33.

115 Andre Comte-Sponville, *A Small Treatise on the Great Virtues* (New York: Henry Holt and Company, 2001), 93.

116 Carlos Bravo, "Jesus of Nazareth, Christ the Liberator," from *Mysterium Liberations: Fundamental Concepts of Liberation Theology*, Ignacio Ellacuria and Jon Sabrino, eds. (Maryknoll, NY: Orbis Books, 1993), 425.

117 Bravo, "Jesus of Nazareth, Christ the Liberator," 95.

118   Comte-Sponville, *A Small Treatise on the Great Virtues*, 101. For more on Benedict de Spinoza, see *A Spinoza Reader: The Ethics and Other Works*, Edwin Curley, ed. and trans. (Princeton, NJ: Princeton University Press, 1994).

119   Comte-Sponville, *A Small Treatise on the Great Virtues*, 102.

120   Comte-Sponville, *A Small Treatise on the Great Virtues*, 94–95. The quote is from *The Philosophical Writings of Descartes*, J. Cottingham, R. Stoothoff, and D. Murdoch, trans. (Cambridge, UK: Cambridge University Press, 1985–1991, Vol. I, art. 156), 385.

121   I am indebted to Sherry Connolly, Founding Director of the Centre for Spirituality at Work, Toronto, Canada, for sending me this gift list.

122   "Global Translations of the Act of Volunteering," *Edmonton Journal*, June 1, 2005.

123   Jean Maalouf, *The Healing Power of Kindness* (Ottawa: Novalis).

124   Ann Meyer, "Spiritual Beliefs Blend into Work," *Chicago Tribune*, January 3, 2005, 3.

125   From *Part One: Life of Emily Dickinson*, #VI, http://www.bartleby.com/113/1006.html (accessed February 11, 2009).

126   Catherine Carson, "Virtual Volunteers Fill the Digital Void, " *Edmonton Journal*, June 1, 2005, EJ12. See also Melanie Collison's article "Philanthropy's Next Generation" in the same issue, on "venture philanthropists." Social Venture Partners Calgary is a partner-driven organization based on the business principles of venture capital (www.svpcalgary.org).

127   Confucius, *Analects*.

128   See Samuel Powell, *A Theology of Christian Spirituality* (Nashville, TN: Abingdon Press, 2005), chapter 9: "Works of Love: Generosity and Justice."

129   By Gregory A. Pierce from "Faith and Work in Cyberspace," November 20, 2006. This online connection has migrated, as of February 2009, to: V1.mycatholicvoice.com/group/faith+and+work+in+cyberspace.

130   Ann Meyer, *Chicago Tribune*, January 3, 2005. To read the full article, see http://www.yale.edu/faith/news/ct-20050103.html (accessed February 11, 2009).

131   Lisa Katz, "Honorable Ways to Give Charity," http://judaism.about.com/od/beliefs/a/charity_nine.htm (accessed February 11, 2009). See also "A Contemporary Reading of Maimonides' Eight Levels," by Jeffrey Spitzer, http://www.myjewishlearning.com/daily_life/Tzedakah/TO_Tzedakah_H_and_D/Tzedakah_J_Trad/Jeff_on_Maimo_8_levels.htm (accessed February 11, 2009).

132   Samyutta Nikaya III.19.

133   Bill Prior, "The Virtue of Generosity: How Can We Define Generosity as a Virtue?" Santa Clara University, Santa Clara, California, Bannan Institute.

134   "Creating a Moral Biography of Wealth: A Conversation with Paul G. Schervish" (The White Papers: Merrill Lynch, Spring 2005).

135   "Creating a Moral Biography of Wealth: A Conversation with Paul G. Schervish."

136   "Creating a Moral Biography of Wealth: A Conversation with Paul G. Schervish."

137   Comte-Sponville, *A Small Treatise on the Great Virtues*, 102.

Chapter 8

138 See my book *God of Many Loves* (Notre Dame, IN: Ave Maria Press, 2001), chapter 4, "The Freeing Love of God," for a fuller explanation of this prayer.

139 http://www.newadvent.org/cathen/06689x.htm (accessed February 11, 2009).

140 http://womenshistory.about.com/cs/quotes/a/qu_e_roosevelt.htm (accessed February 11, 2009).

141 David Whyte, *The Heart Aroused: Poetry and the Preservation of the Soul in Corporate America* (New York: Doubleday Currency, 1994), 39. See also my books *God of Many Loves*, chapter 6, "A Pilgrimage to Deeper Healing," and *The Masculine Spirit* (Ave Maria Press, 1997), chapter 7, "Dealing with Father Wounds" (emotional wounds one received from one's father or mother or some other significant adult figure).

142 See David Irvine, *Becoming Real: Journey to Authenticity* (Sanford, FL: DC Press, 2003).

143 http://www.andrewcohen.org/andrew/authentic-leadership.asp (accessed February 11, 2009).

144 Rosemary Radford Ruether, "Courage as a Christian Virtue," *Cross Currents*, Spring 1983, 8.

145 Cicero, *DeOfficiis*, Book I, No. 20.

146 For an interesting treatment on whistle blowing, see Jeffrey Seglin's online "The Right Thing" column, September 18, 2005 (distributed by the New York Times Syndicate: rightthing@nytimes.com). Jeffrey Seglin is an associate professor at Emerson College, Boston, where he teaches writing and ethics. See also the National Whistleblower Center's website, www.whistleblowers.org.

147 Comte-Sponville, *A Small Treatise on the Great Virtues*, 58–59.

148 Jeffrey MacDonald, "Mixed Signals on the Virtue of Courage," Religion and Ethics, *The Christian Science Monitor*, July 20, 2005.

149 Gula, *Reason Informed by Faith*, 16–17.

150 Oliva, *The Masculine Spirit*, 51. For information on the Amazon archetype, see Christina Spahn's article "Images of the Feminine" in the journal *Radical Grace*, August–September 1991.

151 James F. Keenan, S.J., *Moral Wisdom: Lessons and Texts from the Catholic Tradition* (Lanham, MD: Rowman & Littlefield, 2004), 146–47.

152 Max Oliva, S.J., "Facing Our Fears in the Call to Act Justly," *Spirituality Today*, Vol. 37, No. 3, Fall 1985.

153 An excellent resource is Hank Shea, "Top 10 List: Lessons Learned from White-Collar Criminals," *St. Thomas Lawyer* (Winter 2008), 12–16. Mr. Shea is a Special Assistant U.S. attorney and a Fellow at the University of St. Thomas School of Law in Minneapolis, Minnesota.

154 http://www.usconstitution.net/dream.html (accessed February 11, 2009).

155 Robert Kennedy, "A Tiny Ripple of Hope," Day of Affirmation Address at Cape Town University, June 6, 1966. For a copy of his speech, go to American Rhetoric On-line Speech Bank: http://www.americanrhetoric.com/speeches/rfkcapetown.htm (accessed February 11, 2009).

156 http://nobelprize.org/nobel_prizes/peace/laureates/1991/kyi-bio.html (accessed February 11, 2009).

157 http://www.thesullivanfoundation.org/gsp/principles/gsp/default.asp (accessed February 11, 2009).

158 http://www.thesullivanfoundation.org/gsp/principles/gsp/default.asp (accessed February 11, 2009).

Chapter 9

159 Matthew, Mark, and Luke descriptions of events contain many similar passages, whereas John's Gospel differs greatly from all three. See the Oxford Dictionary, 1991 edition, 1467.

160 Donald L. Gelpi, S.J., *The Firstborn of Many: A Christology for Converting Christians*, Vol. 2 (Milwaukee, WI: Marquette University Press, 2001), 557.

161 H. Richard Niebuhr, *Christ and Culture* (New York: Harper Torchbooks, 1951), 73.

162 Spohn, *Go and Do Likewise*, 66. See also Thomas Rausch, *Who Is Jesus: An Introduction to Christology* (Collegeville, MN: Liturgical Press, 2003), chapter 5.

163 Elizabeth A. Johnson, *Consider Jesus: Waves of Renewal in Christology* (New York: Crossroad, 1990), 51–52.

164 Spohn, *Go and Do Likewise*, 84.

165 Gelpi, *The Firstborn of Many*, 558. See also John Dalla Costa, *Magnificence at Work: Living Faith in Business* (Toronto: Novalis, 2005), chapter 6, "Perspective."

166 The term "non-kingdom moments" was coined by Sr. Karla Felix-Rivera, VDMF.

167 http://www.islam101.com/dawah/pillars.html (accessed February 11, 2009).

168 Marianne Williamson, *A Return to Love* (New York: Harper Collins, 1992), 190–91.

169 Abraham Joshua Heschel, *I Asked for Wonder: A Spiritual Anthology* (New York: Crossroad Publishing, 1983).

170 Johnson, *Consider Jesus*, 52.

Appendix A

171 Thomas Merton, Thomas Keating, Basil Pennington, and John Main are Christian authors who have written about centering prayer. To explore this type of prayer more deeply, you may want to read their works on the subject.

Appendix B

172 I am indebted to Fr. Armand Nigro, S.J., for his pioneer work in this method of prayer.

Appendix D

173 For a fuller explanation of this prayer, see Oliva, *God of Many Loves*, chapter 4.

    This book has been printed on 100% post consumer waste paper, certified Eco-logo and processed chlorine free.